PROGRAMMING LASER PRINTERS

HP AND COMPATIBLES

Timothy Perrin

MIS: *PRESS*

MANAGEMENT INFORMATION SOURCE, INC.

COPYRIGHT

DEDICATION

To my kids, Wendy and Tom. Your patience with me as a father is much greater than my ability has deserved.

TABLE OF CONTENTS

DISK ORDER FORM
ON LAST PAGE
OF BOOK

LIST OF HP COMPATIBLE PRINTERS

Compatible printers include the following:

- Advanced Technologies Laserprint 870, Laserprint 880, CDS 2300, 1570 DW3, 1570 DW2

- Ast TurboLaser/EL

- BDS 630/8

- Blaser Industries BlaserStar

- C. Itoh Jet-Setter

- CIE LIPS 10 Plus

- Data Technology CrystalPrint VIII

- Dataproducts LZR-1230

- Destiny Laser Act I

- Epson GQ-3500

- Genicom Centronics PagePrinter 8, Genicom 5010

- Hewlett-Packard LaserJet series II

- Kyocera F-1000 A, F-2010, F-3010

- Laser Connection PS Jet

- Mannesmann Tally MT910

- NEC Silentwriter LC-890

- OASYS LaserPro Express Series II, LaserPro 810-R, LaserPro Silver Express, LaserPro Gold Express, LaserPro 1510-R

- Okidata Laserline 6

continued...

- Personal Computer Products LaserImage 1000, LaserImage 2000, LaserImage 3000

- Printronix L1012

- QMS Smartwriter 80 Plus, Smartwriter 150, QMS-PS 800, QMS-PS 800+

- Quadram Quadlaser Plus, Quadlaser Forms Printer, Quadlaser PostScript, Quadlaser PostScript Plus, Quadlaser Forms Printer Plus

- Qume LaserTEN, LaserTen Plus, ScripTEN

- Ricoh PC Laser 6000

- Talaris 810, Talaris 812G

- Texas Instruments OmniLaser 2108, OmniLaser 2115

- Toshiba Pagelaser 12

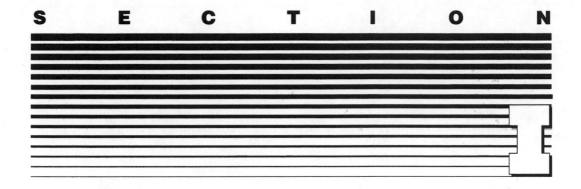

S E C T I O N

1

GETTING STARTED

WHAT THIS BOOK COVERS

This book is about programming the Hewlett-Packard LaserJet+ and compatible laser printers (see list on page ix), including the HP LaserJet Series II.

This book is *not* a user manual or technical reference for a particular printer. It does not discuss how to add toner or how to replace the photosensitive drum, belt, or charge corona unit.

In other words, this book is about software — not hardware.

ASSUMPTIONS

This book is based on the following assumptions:

- You are using a Hewlett-Packard LaserJet+ or compatible laser printer (see list on page ix) connected to an IBM PC or compatible microcomputer. This book does not cover Apple LaserWriters or other laser printers that do not respond to the same commands as the LaserJet+, and it does not discuss using the LaserJet+ with computers that do not run under the MS-DOS and PC-DOS operating systems.

- You know the fundamentals of computer programming in BASIC. Microsoft's QuickBASIC version 4.0 was used for the examples in this book, but if you know any variation of BASIC, the examples should make sense.

HOW THIS BOOK IS ORGANIZED

The book includes 18 chapters and five appendices:

- Chapter 1 explains the general LaserJet command structure.

- Chapter 2 covers the three types of fonts available on LaserJet+ compatible laser printers and explains how they are stored.

- Chapter 3 shows you how to access fonts with commands.

- Chapter 4 provides the information you need to design and download your own custom fonts.

- Chapter 5 explains how you can move to any location on a page quickly and easily.

- Chapter 6 outlines the LaserJet +'s vertical motion commands.

- Chapter 7 outlines the LaserJet +'s horizontal motion commands.

- Chapter 8 lists the commands for setting margins on a page.

- Chapters 9 and 10 explain the two methods of producing graphics with the LaserJet +.

- Chapter 11 explains time-saving macros for producing complicated patterns with simple commands.

- Chapter 12 lists miscellaneous general commands.

- Chapter 13 is a guide to alternative laser printers.

- Chapters 14 and 15 provide tips on how to get the most out of a LaserJet with two popular word processing packages: WordPerfect and Microsoft Word.

- Chapters 16 and 17 provide tips on how to use the LaserJet + with the top two PC desktop publishing programs: PageMaker and Ventura Publisher.

- Chapter 18 tells you about various other software packages for LaserJet + compatible printers.

The appendices cover general technical information. If you have trouble understanding technical discussions in this book, refer to the appropriate appendix.

HOW TO USE THIS BOOK

This book is designed to be read sequentially. You will find the entire book — as well as individual chapters — more informative if you read the chapters from beginning to end.

Most chapters begin with a short explanation of the theories behind the topics covered in that chapter. If you start at the beginning of each chapter, you will better understand important concepts.

Because you may want to refer to a particular section for specific information, some important material is repeated in several chapters.

This book covers much technical material. If you become confused, read another three or four paragraphs; often, your questions will be answered. If you are still lost, turn to the appendices for clarification. Appendix A is an introduction to computer mathematics; Appendix B explains terms such as bits, bytes, and ASCII, and Appendix C lists the ASCII codes. Appendix D covers symbols sets, and Appendix E lists sample programs.

CONVENTIONS

This book uses several command conventions.

Text in the following typeface,

```
C:\LJFONTS>
```

is text that your computer writes on the screen. Text you type on the keyboard appears in this typeface:

```
MAKEPRD
```

Keys to be pressed are indicated in square brackets:

[Esc]
[Alt]

[Return] refers to the key marked "Enter" or "Return" or marked with an arrow that points down and to the left (⏎).

When two keys are separated by a slash,

[Shift/F7]

you are to hold down the first key and simultaneously press the second key.

When there are spaces between keys,

[Esc] [t]

you are to press them in sequence. In the above example, you would press and release the ESC key and then press the "t" key.

Text in the following format,

<u>ESC</u> *k # H

indicates a command sequence — a set of characters that instructs the printer to perform a task.

If characters are underlined, such as <u>ESC</u>, they represent a single command character with a special name. For example, <u>ESC</u> is the character called escape, which is generated when you press the ESC key.

Note the difference between l — the lowercase letter "L," and 1 — the number one (with the small downward hook at the top). Also, note that 0 — the number zero — is narrow and tall, while O — the uppercase letter "O" — is wide.

Numbers

The variety of number systems used by computers can sometimes become confusing. For the most part, this book uses the decimal (base 10) number system; however, it sometimes uses the hexadecimal (base 16) number system (see Appendix A for an explanation of these systems). If there is a possibility of confusion about which number system is in use, a subscript D will follow decimal numbers, as in 15$_D$, and a subscript H will follow hexadecimal numbers, for example, 0A$_H$.

ASCII characters that would normally print are shown as they would print, such as A, B, or C. In cases where you might confuse the printable ASCII characters 0-9 with decimal or hexadecimal numbers, they will be followed by a subscript A, as in 8$_A$.

Spaces in Commands

You control a printer with commands comprised of printing and non-printing characters. The next chapter explains the basic command structure.

You will find spaces in all command sequences that are more than one character long. Spaces make the commands easier to read. As a result, the command

<u>ESC</u>(8U<u>ESC</u>(s0p10h12v0s3b3T

is listed as

<u>ESC</u> (8U <u>ESC</u> (s 0p 10h 12v 0s 3b 3T

When sending commands to the printer, *do not* send any spaces unless the command explicitly calls for them with the symbol **SPACE**.

For more information on number and spacing conventions, see Chapter 1. You may also want to refer to the appendices, which explain such topics as ASCII codes and how computers handle numbers.

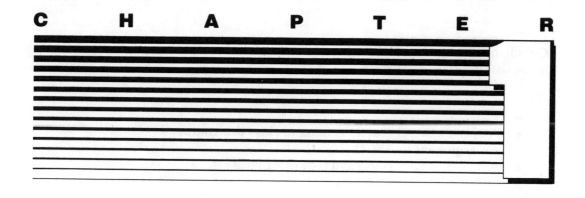

CHAPTER

LASERJET + COMMAND SYNTAX

Commands for the Hewlett-Packard LaserJet+ and compatible printers general-ly consist of four components:

- ESC
- A one- or two-character **command class** designator
- An **argument** in ASCII
- A one-character **command type** designator

For example, the command to set the left margin to column 20 is

ESC &a 20 L

In this command, &a is the command class designator, 20 is the argument, and L is the command type designator.

The command for setting the right margin to column 70 is

ESC &a 70 M

This time, &a is again the command class designator, 70 is the argument, and M is the command type designator.

COMBINING COMMANDS

You may combine LaserJet+ commands that have the same command class desig-nators. When you combine commands, you need ESC and the command class only once, at the beginning of the sequence. Only the last command type should be in uppercase. All other command types should be in lowercase.

For example, you can combine the command to set the left margin to column 20 with the command to set the right margin to column 70 as follows:

ESC &a 20 l 70 M

ARGUMENTS

An **argument** is a number that tells a command "how much." On an HP Laser-Jet+, arguments are almost always in printable ASCII characters.

For example, in the command

ESC &a 20 L

20 is the argument. The general form of that command is

ESC &a # L

The command says "set the left margin at column #." Whatever you substitute for # is the argument.

On an HP LaserJet+, arguments are almost always in ASCII characters; thus, if you want to set the left margin in column 20, you send the characters 2 and 0 to the printer as the argument.

CATEGORIES OF COMMANDS

The LaserJet+ command structure is part of Hewlett-Packard's Printer Control Language (PCL). At first glance, it may seem a bit convoluted and overly complicated, but after you become familiar with it, the structure is extremely well organized and logical. Laser printers perform so many more tasks than regular printers that a new control language was needed.

PCL divides printer commands into eight categories:

- Font Selection and Control
- Direct Print Positioning
- Vertical Motion
- Horizontal Motion
- Page Formatting
- Graphics
- Macros
- Miscellaneous Commands

These commands are explained in detail in the following chapters.

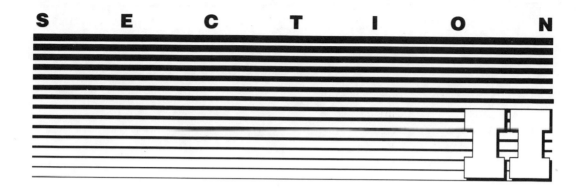

S E C T I O N

II

FONTS ON THE LASERJET +

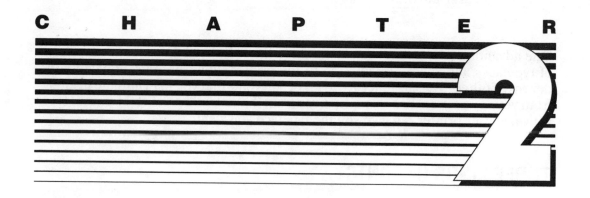

C H A P T E R

2

HOW THE
LASERJET + STORES FONTS

One advantage of a LaserJet+ compatible printer is the ability to print a variety of typefaces and styles. In addition to the printer's built-in fonts, you can add dozens of others by using font cartridges or soft fonts that you load into the printer from your computer. For example, if you want 8-point bold print or 14-point Helvetica, a laser printer can give you the typeface you want.

THREE KINDS OF FONTS

LaserJet+ compatible printers use three types of fonts:

- internal fonts built into the machine
- cartridge fonts you plug into the machine
- downloaded soft fonts

A laser printer uses its memory to store patterns from which it prints characters. **Internal fonts** and **cartridge fonts** are stored in sections of the printer's ROM (Read Only Memory), while **soft fonts** are stored in the printer's RAM (Random Access Memory). RAM is erased when the printer is turned off, but ROM is permanent. As a result, soft fonts must be reloaded into the printer each time it is turned on.

Internal Fonts

LaserJet and compatible printers include anywhere from two to more than 20 installed internal fonts. Hewlett-Packard offers the least number of built-in fonts — only six in the LaserJet Series II — while some competitors offer two dozen or more.

Font Cartridges

In addition to your printer's built-in fonts, most manufacturers offer a variety of fonts on cartridges. Some LaserJet+ compatible printers can use Hewlett-Packard font cartridges; however, most manufacturers make sure that their printers only work with their cartridges.

The specifics of installing font cartridges vary from printer to printer. See your printer's user manual.

Soft Fonts

LaserJet+ compatible printers can also use soft fonts downloaded to the printer from a disk. A number of fonts from many companies are available. On a per-font basis, soft fonts are much cheaper than font cartridges. The only problem is that you must download them to the printer each time you turn it on.

You can also design custom fonts to suit particular needs. Chapter 4 explains how to design your own fonts.

FONT HEADERS

In the printer's memory, each font has a font descriptor or **header** containing information about the entire font. The header lists the following characteristics of a font:

- orientation
- symbol set
- spacing
- pitch
- height
- style (italics)
- stroke weight (boldness)
- typeface

When the computer instructs the printer to select a particular font, the printer checks the characteristics specified by the font descriptor for each available font and selects the one that most closely matches the font requested.

Orientation

Orientation refers to the direction in which the print travels on the page. **Portrait orientation** means text runs across the paper's narrow dimension; **landscape orientation** means the text runs across the paper's wide dimension.

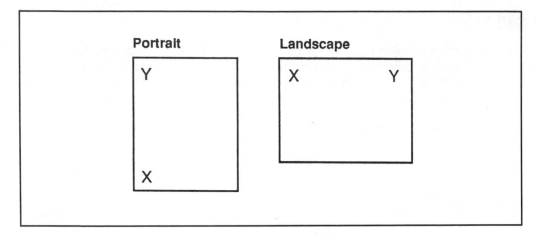

Figure 2.1   *Portrait and Landscape Orientations*

Origin

The **origin** is the upper left corner of the page (see Figure 2.1), from which all margins are measured. Y is the origin in portrait mode; X is the origin in landscape mode.

Default Orientation

When the printer is first turned on, its default setting is usually portrait orientation. On most LaserJet+ compatible laser printers, this default can be changed using a combination of front-panel switches or software commands; however, this process varies from machine to machine.

Font Orientation

Laser printer fonts each have a normal orientation, either portrait or landscape. On the LaserJet, you must have access to a font in the correct orientation to print text in that orientation. For example, if all your fonts are portrait-oriented, you won't be able to print in landscape mode.

Several LaserJet clones have worked around this limitation. For example, Mannesmann Tally's MT910 laser printer automatically rotates any font to print in either orientation. All you must do is issue the command for an orientation change; the printer takes care of the rest.

Symbol Sets

A **symbol set** is the arrangement of characters in a font. While most fonts are built around the ASCII standard (see Appendices B and C), some fonts contain special characters such as international characters, line-drawing characters, or mathematical symbols.

Three of the most common symbol sets are USASCII, Roman Extended, and Roman-8. USASCII contains the standard ASCII characters (see Appendices B and C). Roman Extended contains a group of international characters. Roman-8 is a combination of the two. Following are the characters in these symbol sets.

!"#$%&()*+,-./0123456789:;< = >?@
ABCDEFGHIJKLMNOPQRSTUVWXYZ[\]^_`
abcdefghijklmnopqrstuvwxyz{|}~

USASCII

ÀÂÈÊËÎÏ´`ˆ¨˜ÙÛ£¯ °ÇçÑñ¡¿¤£¥§ƒ¢êô
ûáéóúàèòùäëöüÅîØÆåíøæÄìÖÜÉïßÔÁÃã
ÐđÎÓÒÕõŠšÚŸÿÞþ —¼½ªº«■»±

Roman Extended

!"#$%&()*+,-./0123456789:;< = >?@
ABCDEFGHIJKLMNOPQRSTUVWXYZ[\]^_`
abcdefghijklmnopqrstuvwxyz{|}~
ÀÂÈÊËÎÏ´`ˆ¨˜ÙÛ£¯ °ÇçÑñ¡¿¤£¥§ƒ¢êô
ûáéóúàèòùäëöüÅîØÆåíøæÄìÖÜÉïßÔÁÃã
ÐđÎÓÒÕõŠšÚŸÿÞþ —¼½ªº«■»±

Roman-8

Figure 2.2   *Symbol Set Characters*

On the LaserJet+, you must have a font with the correct symbol set in order to use any of the special characters. Some LaserJet+ clones, however, can change a font in the Roman-8 symbol set into a font with a foreign symbol set by substituting the appropriate international characters for the standard ASCII characters. See the chart in Appendix D for the substitutions in the main international symbol sets.

Spacing

Spacing refers to the horizontal distance allotted to each character on a line. There are two types of spacing: proportional and fixed.

This book is set in a proportionally spaced font. In a proportional font, each character takes up only as much space as it needs, so a W is wider than an i, for example. To illustrate, the following example includes ten of each character:

WWWWWWWWWW
iiiiiiiiii

In a fixed-space font, each character is allocated the same amount of space regardless of its width. The following example shows ten W's and ten i's in a fixed-space font (Courier).

```
WWWWWWWWWW
iiiiiiiiii
```

Pitch

The pitch of a font is the distance between characters for fixed-space fonts or the width of the <u>SPACE</u> character for proportionally spaced fonts. For example, in a 10-pitch fixed-space font, each character is 1/10" wide. In a 10-pitch proportionally spaced font, the <u>SPACE</u> character produces a blank space 1/10" wide, while the width of other characters varies.

Height

The height of a font is the distance from the bottom of one line to the bottom of the next line, measured in points (72 points = 1").

This line is in 8-point type.

This line is in 10-point type.

This line is in 12-point type.

Extra space between lines is called **leading** (pronounced LED-ing). Before phototypesetting and desktop publishing, type was printed from lead ingots. To help a fixed amount of text fill the available space, printers inserted thin strips of lead between lines of type. Leading does not affect type size — only line spacing.

Style

The style of a font is either upright or *italic*.

Stroke Weight

On a Laserjet+, each font has a stroke weight (boldness) rating from 7 to +7. Normal weight type has a weight of 0.

This typeface is normal weight.

This bold typeface has a weight of +3.

Typeface

On a LaserJet +, the term **typeface** describes the design of the character's family, such as Courier, Times Roman, or Helvetica.

`This line is in a Courier typeface.`

This line is in a Times Roman typeface.

This line is in a Helvetica typeface.

INDIVIDUAL CHARACTERS

In the printer's memory, each font resides in 256 memory slots. Each slot contains the dot pattern for one character.

Low Memory

The characters stored in slots 00 to 127 are fairly standard. In most symbol sets, they are characters established by the American Standard Code for Information Interchange (ASCII). In the ASCII code, slot 65 always contains the letter A; slot 118 always contains the letter v; and so on. The control codes — from slots 00 to 31 — generally do not print; instead, they control the printer. Most printers, however, have special commands to access characters stored in these memory locations. The memory slots that hold the ASCII characters are referred to as **low memory**.

Fonts that fit entirely into low memory are referred to as **7-bit** fonts because seven bits are enough to designate 128 characters. (See Appendix B for an explanation of bits and bytes.)

Some symbol sets do not use the ASCII standard characters. Foreign language symbol sets often substitute a few special characters for standard ASCII characters (see Appendix D). Other symbol sets depart from the ASCII standard entirely; the character assigned to 65 — rather than being the letter "A" or even α (the Greek Alpha) — may be something completely unrelated, such as √.

High Memory

While there is at least some order in low memory, in high memory (slots 128 to 255), anarchy reins. Over the years, various printer manufacturers have insisted on using their own character sets. IBM printers use a set of international and line-drawing characters. Epson settled on italic versions of the characters found in low memory. For the most part, Hewlett-Packard places the Roman-extended character set in high memory.

Fonts that store characters in high memory are **8-bit** fonts because they need all eight bits to allow for more than 128 characters. (See Appendices B and C.)

Putting Theory into Practice

The ability of LaserJet+ compatibles to handle fonts quickly and easily is one of their greatest assets. If you have enough memory, you can work with up to 32 fonts at a time. You will see in the next two chapters just how to store, select, and create fonts for your laser printer.

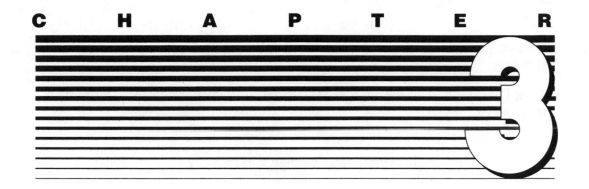

C H A P T E R

3

SELECTING AND CONTROLLING FONTS

This chapter details the commands that instruct the printer to use a particular font.

On a LaserJet+ or compatible printer, you can use commands to select fonts in three ways:

- by switching between fonts designated as primary and secondary
- by description
- by font ID number

PRIMARY AND SECONDARY FONTS

The first method of font selection on a LaserJet+ or compatible printer is to designate two fonts as primary and secondary and switch between them with simple commands almost any word processor can handle. This technique allows older programs that have limited ability to control the printer—such as WordStar—to take greater advantage of a LaserJet+ compatible.

When you first select a font by description (see the next section of this chapter), you designate it as **primary** or **secondary**. Using a left parenthesis when selecting a font by description establishes that font as the primary font. Using a right parenthesis makes the font secondary. For example, the command ESC (8U selects a font with the Roman-8 character set as the primary font, while ESC) 8U selects it as the secondary font.

Switching between Primary and Secondary Fonts

Once the primary and secondary fonts are selected, the following one-character commands will switch back and forth between the fonts.

Command	Explanation
SI	select primary font
SO	select secondary font

Example of Primary/Secondary Font Selection

This short program demonstrates how you can switch between the primary and secondary fonts. It assumes that you have already defined the primary and secondary fonts.

```
LPRINT CHR$(15)                    ' SI - SELECT PRIMARY
                                   ' FONT
LPRINT "This is printed in the primary font."
LPRINT CHR$(14)                    ' SO - SELECT SECONDARY
                                   ' FONT
LPRINT "This is printed in the secondary font."
END
```

Why Use Primary/Secondary Fonts?

You will rarely want to use the primary/secondary font system. Hewlett-Packard included the system in the original LaserJet so it could support earlier word processing programs such as WordStar. Most of the time, you will select fonts by description.

SELECTING FONTS BY DESCRIPTION

To select a font by description, you must tell the printer the characteristics of the font you need. The printer then searches the headers of the fonts available in the font pool and selects the font that most closely matches your request.

Font Characteristics

As mentioned in Chapter 2, the following characteristics describe a font. They will be discussed in detail in this chapter.

- orientation
- symbol set
- print spacing
- print pitch
- character height
- style (italics)
- stroke weight (boldness)
- typeface

Sample Font Description Command

A complete font description sequence resembles the following:

ESC &l 0 R   ESC (8U ESC (s 0p 10h 12v 0s 0b 3T

ESC &l 0 R specifies portrait orientation. ESC is the escape character that begins most commands to the printer. &l is the command class. 0 is the argument that specifies portrait orientation (1 would specify landscape orientation). R is the command-type designator. ESC (8U selects the Roman-8 symbol set.

The next part of the command specifies all remaining font characteristics in a single, combined command sequence. ESC (s is the escape character and the command class. 0p selects fixed spacing. 10h specifies a 10-pitch font (10 characters per inch). 12v indicates a 12-point font. 0s chooses an upright (non-italic) font. 0b indicates a font with a medium stroke weight. Finally, 3T indicates a Courier font.

Remember, *do not* send the spaces in the example font description sequences to the printer.

Specifying Only Changing Characteristics

A complete font selection command specifies all eight font characteristics; however, if the font you are selecting has a particular characteristic that is the same as the current font, you need not specify that characteristic.

For example, if you send the font selection command used in the previous section and then want to select another font with portrait orientation, it is not necessary to specify the orientation again.

In other words, the printer assumes you want the same trait unless you tell it otherwise.

Priority System

Font selection by description works on a priority basis. The printer examines each characteristic in the order discussed previously and selects the fonts that fit each element of the description. Other fonts are not considered. When the printer reaches the end of the list, it will determine the font that most closely matches the description you have provided.

On some compatible printers, fonts can be modified to fit a font description. For example, the printer may automatically create a bold version of a font if one is requested, or it may slant the font to create an italic version.

Priority System Example

Suppose you have the following fonts loaded in your printer:

	Font 1	Font 2	Font 3	Font 4
Orientation:	portrait	portrait	portrait	portrait
Symbol Set:	Roman-8	USASCII	USASCII	USASCII
Spacing:	proportional	proportional	fixed	proportional
Pitch:	10	10	17	10
Height:	12 pt	12 pt	8 pt	12 pt
Style:	upright	upright	upright	italic
Weight:	normal	normal	normal	normal
Typeface:	TMS RMN	TMS RMN	HELV	HELV

Suppose you send a command to the printer to select a font with the following characteristics:

Orientation:	portrait
Symbol Set:	USASCII
Spacing:	proportional
Pitch:	10
Height:	12 pt
Style:	upright
Weight:	normal
Typeface:	HELV

The printer first examines the orientation of the fonts in the font pool. Because all fonts are of portrait orientation, all survive the first cut.

The printer then examines the symbol sets of available fonts. Font 1 is eliminated from consideration because it contains the wrong symbol set. The requested font should have the USASCII symbol set, and font 1 has the Roman-8 symbol set.

Font 3 is discarded next because it has fixed spacing, and the requested font should have proportional spacing.

Fonts 2 and 4 remain. Both fonts have the right pitch and the right height. Font 4, however, is an italic font, and the requested font should be upright; thus, when the printer examines the style of the fonts, it discards font 4, leaving only font 2. Note that font 2 has the wrong typeface. Style (such as italic) is a higher priority than typeface to a LaserJet+, and font 2 is selected.

Suppose you specified a font with the following characteristics:

Orientation:	portrait
Symbol Set:	USASCII
Spacing:	proportional
Pitch:	14
Height:	10 pt
Style:	italic
Weight:	normal
Typeface:	Gothic

Font 4 would be selected. Fonts 2 and 4 match the first three traits. Neither font matches the pitch or height specification, so neither font is a closer fit than the other. At the style level, the final cut is made. Font 4 has italic style, and font 2 is upright. Font 4 is selected.

FONT SELECTION COMMANDS

The following sections describe each of the font selection commands.

Page Orientation

Orientation refers to the direction in which print runs across the page. Refer to Chapter 2 for a full explanation of portrait and landscape orientation.

<u>Command</u>	<u>Explanation</u>
<u>ESC</u> &l # O	# = 0 (portrait orientation) # = 1 (landscape orientation)

On the LaserJet + (but not on all compatibles), when you issue the command to print in landscape mode, you must have a landscape font available. On the standard LaserJet +, the only landscape font is the tiny Line Printer font, useful primarily for printing spreadsheets. To print anything else in landscape mode, you will need font cartridges or downloaded fonts.

Some compatibles automatically rotate fonts so they can print in landscape orientation, which is a very useful capability. Never count on this feature, however, when programming for a variety of printers.

Forced Page Print

Always issue the command to select orientation at the beginning of a page. Issuing this command at the beginning forces a page to close and print, ejecting the page currently in the printer.

Example of Orientation Command

The following short program selects a font with landscape orientation:

```
E$ = CHR$(27)              ' DEFINE ESCAPE LPRINT
E$;"&l0R"                  ' CALL FOR LANDSCAPE
                           ' ORIENTATION
END
```

Orientation and Margins

When you change orientation, the origin changes. Remember, the origin is the point at which the printer starts printing.

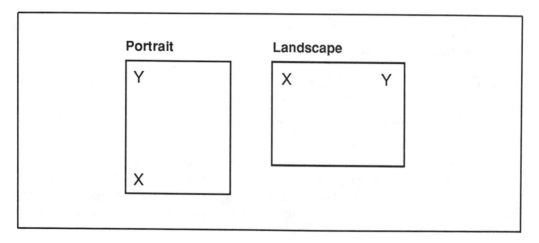

Figure 3.1   Portrait and Landscape Orientation (same as Figure 2.1)

Y is the origin in portrait orientation, and X is the origin in landscape orientation (see Figure 3.1). If nothing has been printed on that page, the printer margins also change to the new orientation before printing. If any text has already been printed on a page, printer margins do not change until the next page.

Printer margins are margins that are set with commands to the printer and not handled by software on the computer. Most word processors handle a left margin by sending a series of spaces to the printer before sending the first character on the line; these spaces make up a software margin. You can, however, set the margin in the printer by sending it a Margin Set command (see Chapter 8, "Page Formatting").

For example, if you set the top and bottom printer margins at 1/2" and the left and right printer margins at 1", they will remain in effect for both portrait and landscape modes. When printing in landscape orientation, however, the top margin runs down the long dimension of the page.

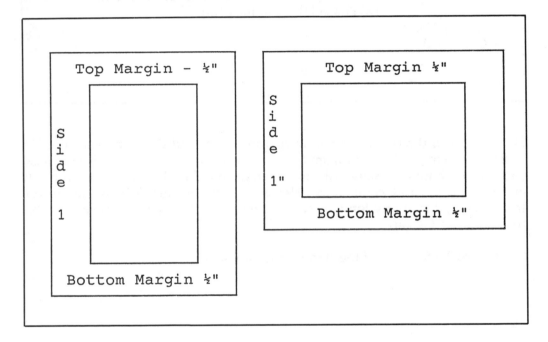

Figure 3.2   *Margins in Portrait and Landscape Orientations*

Symbol Sets

Symbol sets differ in the characters that occupy various printer memory locations. For example, the memory location associated with the letter C in the USASCII symbol set is filled by the Greek letter Gamma — Γ — in the Math-8 symbol set.

Command	Explanation
Primary Font: ESC ({code}	{code} specifies the symbol set for the font you want. (The curly brackets are not part of the command. Don't send them to the printer.)
Secondary Font: ESC) {code}	

Hewlett-Packard has defined nearly 20 symbol sets and the commands used to designate them. Other font manufacturers, however, have assigned symbol set commands without any standard; thus, when you buy downloadable fonts, you may encounter conflicting commands. However, don't let this fact discourage you from buying third-party fonts; they are often much better than those available from Hewlett-Packard.

See Figure 3.3 for a list of the standard symbol sets.

Symbol Set	Code	Symbol Set	Code
8-bit Symbol Sets		**7-bit Symbol Sets**	
Roman-8	8U	ASCII JIS	0K
Kana-8	8K	ASCII US	0U
Math-8	8M	Chinese ISO	2K
ANSI/Windows	9U	Norwegian ISO v1	0D
PC-8	10U	Norwegian ISO v2	1D
Denmark/Norway PC-8	11U	English	1E
		English 2	2E
Non-Alphabetic Symbol Sets		French ISO	0F
		French ISO 2	1F
Line Draw	0B	German HP	0G
Math Symbols	0A	German ISO	1G
Matha	0Q	IRV	2U
Mathb	1Q	Italian	0I
Math7	0M	Japanese	1J
PiFont	15Q	Latin ISO	0N
PiFonta	2Q	Portuguese ISO/IBM	5S
OCR-A	0O	Portuguese ISO	4S
OCR-B	1O	Roman Extension	0E
Bar 3 of 9	0Y	Spanish HP	1S
EAN/UPC	8Y	Spanish ISO/IBM	6S
		ISO	2S
		Swedish	3S
		Swedish/Finnish	0S
		US Legal	1U

Figure 3.3   *Symbol Set Codes*

Appendix D contains a translation table showing which characters differ in many of these symbol sets.

Example of Font Selection

The following short program selects a primary font with the Roman-8 character set:

```
E$ = CHR$(27)              ' DEFINE ESCAPE
LPRINT E$;"(8U";           ' CALL FOR ROMAN-8
END
```

Print Spacing

In a proportionally spaced font, wider letters such as "W" are allocated more space on a line than narrow letters such as "i."

Command	Explanation
Primary Font: ESC (s # P	# = 0 asks for a fixed-space font # = 1 asks for a proportionally spaced font
Secondary Font: ESC) s # P	

Example of Selecting Print Spacing Characteristic

The following short program selects fonts with proportional and then fixed spacing:

```
E$ = CHR$(27)                    ' ESCAPE CHARACTER
LPRINT E$;"(s1P"                 ' SELECT PROPORTIONAL
                                 ' SPACING
LPRINT "This is printed in a proportional font."
LPRINT E$;"(s0P"                 ' SELECT FIXED SPACING
LPRINT "This is printed in a fixed-space font."
LPRINT CHR$(12)                  ' FORM FEED
END
```

The following could be the output of that program (depending on your printer's available fonts):

This line is printed in a proportional font.

`This line is printed in a fixed-space font.`

Print Pitch

Pitch is a measure of how many characters the printer prints in each horizontal inch. Typical values for # are 10, 12, or 16.66 characters per inch (CPI). Fonts may have different pitches. On most LaserJet+ compatibles, the default pitch is 10 CPI.

Command	Explanation
Primary Font: ESC (s # H	# is the print pitch in characters per inch.
Secondary Font: ESC)s # H	

If you used the previous command to select a font with a fixed pitch, this command will select a font in which all the characters are the width you request. For example, ESC (s 0P 10H will select a fixed pitch font (0p) that has a pitch of 10 characters per inch (10H).

If you have requested a proportionally spaced font, you need not also specify a print pitch. However, if you do, this command will select a font in which the SPACE character is the width (pitch) you request. For example, ESC (s 1p 10H will select a proportionally spaced font (1p) that has a SPACE character 1/10" wide (10H). The other characters will have varying widths.

Example of Pitch Selection

This short program demonstrates choosing a font with a pitch of 12 characters per inch.

```
E$ = CHR$(27)                    ' ESCAPE CHARACTER
LPRINT E$;"(s12H"                ' SELECT 12 PITCH
LPRINT "This is printed in a 12 pitch font."
LPRINT CHR$(12)                  ' FORM FEED TO EJECT
                                 ' PAGE

END
```

Following is an example of the program's output from a printer with a 12-pitch Prestige font available in the font pool.

```
This is printed in a 12 pitch font.
```

Alternate Command to Set Font Pitch Spacing

The following command provides an alternate way to select font pitch; it requests that both the primary and secondary fonts should have the specified spacing.

Command	Explanation
ESC &k # S	# = 0 sets the spacing for both primary and secondary fonts as 10 characters per inch.
	# = 2 sets the spacing for both the primary and secondary fonts as 16.66 characters per inch.

Remember that because this command has a different command class, it cannot be combined with the other font selection commands.

Example of Alternate Pitch Selection

The following short program indicates that both the primary and secondary fonts should have a pitch of 16.66 CPI.

```
E$ = CHR$(27)                    ' ESCAPE CHARACTER
LPRINT E$;"&k2S"                 ' SELECT 16.66 CPI FOR
                                 ' PRIMARY AND
                                 ' SECONDARY FONTS
LPRINT "This is printed at 16.66 characters per
inch."
LPRINT CHR$(12)                  ' FORM FEED TO EJECT
                                 ' PAGE
END
```

The following example resembles the output of that program:

This is printed at 16.66 characters per inch.

Character Height

The following command selects a font with the specified vertical spacing:

Command	Explanation
Primary Font: ESC (s # V	# is the height of the font in points
Secondary Font: ESC) s # V	

For example, the command **ESC** (s 12 V sets the character height to 12 points. If you select a character height that is not available, the printer selects the font closest in height.

The height of type has been measured in points for hundreds of years. A point is 1/72". Type height is measured from the bottom of one line to the bottom of the next, and the measurement includes the height of the characters *and* the space between lines. Standard 6-line-per-inch type is 12 points high (12/72 = 1/6). Other typical values for font heights are 7 points (10 LPI), 8 points (9 LPI), 8.5 points (8.5 LPI), 10 points (7 LPI), and 14 points (5 LPI).

Example of Font Height Selection

The following short program selects fonts of various heights. While the fonts are different sizes from 8 to 12 points, they are printed on lines of the same height — 18 points. Remember, leading (inter-line spacing) does not affect type size.

The command for setting line spacing, (**ESC** &l # C), is covered in Chapter 6.

```
E$ = CHR$(27)                    ' ESCAPE CHARACTER
FF$ = CHR$(12)                   ' FORM FEED CHARACTER

LPRINT E$;"&l12C";               ' SET LINE SPACING AT
                                 ' 12/48" (18 POINTS)

LPRINT E$;"(s8V";                ' SELECT 8 POINT TYPE
LPRINT "This is printed in 8 point type."

LPRINT E$;"(s10V";               ' SELECT 10 POINT TYPE
LPRINT "This is printed in 10 point type."

LPRINT E$;"(s12V";               ' SELECT 12 POINT TYPE
LPRINT "This is printed in 12 point type."

LPRINT FF$                       ' FORM FEED

END
```

The following is one example of the output of the program (depending on your printer's available fonts):

This is printed in 8 point type.

This is printed in 10 point type.

This is printed in 12 point type.

Style (Italics)

The following command selects either an upright or an *italic* font.

Command	Explanation
Primary Font: ESC (s # S	# = 0 selects an upright font
Secondary Font: ESC) s # S	# = 1 selects an *italic* font

On a LaserJet+, you must have an italic font available in the font pool, or this command will have no effect. On some clones, the printer can automatically italicize a font whenever it fits the rest of the selection criteria.

Example of Italics Selection

The following program selects an italic font:

```
E$ = CIIR$(27)                    ' ESCAPE CHARACTER
LPRINT E$;"(s1S";                 ' SELECT ITALIC FONT
LPRINT "This is an example of italic text."
LPRINT CHR$(12)                   ' FORM FEED
END
```

The following example resembles the output of the program (again, depending on your printer's available fonts):

This is an example of italic text.

Stroke Weight (Boldface)

The following command specifies the weight, or "boldness," of a font.

Command	Explanation
Primary Font ESC (s # B	# is a value from -7 to 7
Secondary Font ESC) s # B	

Use # = 0 for normal-weight type. Use positive numbers (with no + sign) from 1 to 7 for bold type. Use 1 for type only slightly bold and 7 for very bold type. Use negative numbers from -1 to -7 for lighter than normal type. Use -1 for type that is only slightly lighter than normal and -7 for very light type.

Example of Stroke Weight Selection

The following program selects a regular-weight font, a font with a boldness of 3, and, finally, a regular-weight font again.

```
E$ = CHR$(27)                    ' ESCAPE CHARACTER

LPRINT E$;"(s0B";                ' SELECT REGULAR WEIGHT
LPRINT "This is printed in normal weight type."

LPRINT E$;"(s3B";                ' SELECT TYPE WITH
                                 ' WEIGHT = 3
LPRINT "This font has a weight of +3"

LPRINT E$;"(s0B";                ' SELECT REGULAR WEIGHT
                                 ' AGAIN
LPRINT "This font is, again, a normal weight."

LPRINT CHR$(12)                  ' FORM FEED TO EJECT
                                 ' PAGE
END
```

The following example resembles the program's output from a printer with access to fonts with those weights.

This is printed in normal weight type.

This font has a weight of +3.

This font is, again, a normal weight.

Typeface

Typeface is the final characteristic the printer examines when selecting a font.

<u>Command</u>	<u>Explanation</u>
Primary Font: ESC (s # T	# specifies the typeface. (See Figure 3.4.)
Secondary Font: ESC) s # T	

Typeface is the artistic design of the type such as Courier, Times Roman, or Helvetica.

`This line is in a Courier typeface.`

This line is in a Times Roman typeface.

This line is in a Helvetica typeface.

Hewlett-Packard has designated several typeface numbers. Other manufacturers adhere to the Hewlett-Packard standard when producing similar fonts. When producing other typefaces, however, there is no standardization. As long as typeface designations from two different manufacturers don't conflict, there's no problem. If they do, you must modify one of the fonts, using a font-editing program such as FontGen IV (see Chapter 18).

Hewlett-Packard has standardized the typefaces in Figure 3.4:

Value of T	Typeface
0	Line Printer
1	Pica
2	Elite
3	Courier
4	Helvetica (HELV, Swiss)
5	Times Roman, Dutch (TMS RMN)
6	Gothic
7	Script
8	Prestige
9	Caslon
10	Orator
11	Presentation
12	Helvetica Condensed
14	Futura
15	Palatino (Zapf Calligraphic)
16	Souvenir
17	Zapf Humanist (Optima)
18	Garamond
19	Cooper
20	Coronet
21	Broadway
22	Bodoni
23	Century Schoolbook
24	University Roman
25	Avant Garde Gothic
27	Korinna
28	Bitstream Charter
29	Cloister Black
30	Galliard
136	Futura Book
146	Futura Light
148	Helvetica Light

Figure 3.4   *Hewlett-Packard Typeface Designations*

Example of Typeface Selection

This program selects an Optima font, a Courier font, and, finally, a Gothic font.

```
E$ = CHR$(27)                      ' ESCAPE CHARACTER

LPRINT E$;"(s17T";                 ' SELECT OPTIMA TYPEFACE
LPRINT "This is printed in an Optima typeface."

LPRINT E$;"(s0p3T";                ' SELECT COURIER
                                   ' TYPEFACE
                                   ' 0p BECAUSE FIXED PITCH
LPRINT "This is printed in a Courier typeface."

LPRINT E$;"(s6T";                  ' SELECT GOTHIC TYPEFACE
LPRINT "This font is a Gothic typeface."

LPRINT CHR$(12)                    ' FORM FEED
END
```

The program produces the following output:

> This is printed in an Optima typeface.
> This is printed in a Courier typeface.
> This font is a Gothic typeface.

FONT ID NUMBERS

The third way to select and manipulate fonts on a LaserJet+ compatible is by using font ID numbers.

Assigning Font ID Numbers

The following command assigns the number # to a font, where # is the font's identification number.

Command	Explanation
ESC *c # D	Assigns # as the font ID number of the currently selected font. Valid font ID numbers range from 0 to 32767.

Font Numbers for Downloaded Fonts

For downloaded fonts, the command to assign font numbers is the first command of the downloading sequence; therefore, all downloaded fonts automatically have a font number. See Chapter 4, "Downloading Fonts," for details.

Font Numbers for Internal or Cartridge Fonts

There are four steps in assigning a font number to an internal or cartridge font:

1. Use a font description sequence to select the font as the primary font.

2. Send SI to make sure you are using the primary font.

3. Use the command

   ESC *c # D

   to assign the ID number to the font.

4. Use the command

   ESC *c 6F

   to make the font ID number temporary (the font number will be erased by a Reset or Delete All Fonts command) Or use the command

   ESC *c 6f 5F

   to make the font ID number assignment "permanent."

Selecting a Font by ID Number

Once a font has been assigned a font ID number, the following commands select the font with an ID number equal to # as the primary or secondary font.

Command	Explanation
ESC (# X	Select font # as primary font.
ESC) # X	Select font # as secondary font.

Font and Character Control by ID Number

The operation of the following command depends on the value of #:

Command	Explanation
ESC *c # F	# = 0 deletes *all* fonts and deletes all font ID numbers assigned to internal and cartridge fonts.
	# = 1 deletes temporary fonts and temporary font ID numbers assigned to internal and cartridge fonts.
	# = 2 deletes the font with the most recently specified ID number.
	# = 3 deletes the most recently received download character in the font with the most recently specified font ID number.
	# = 4 makes the font with the most recently specified font ID number temporary. Temporary fonts are deleted by a reset command.
	# = 5 makes the font with the most recently specified font ID number permanent. Permanent fonts are not affected by a reset.
	# = 6 assigns the current font ID number to the current font. A font number designated with this command is temporary.

Note: When the printer receives the command to delete a font in use, the current page is printed before the font is deleted. When the command is received to delete a font that is not in use, all pages prior to the current page are printed before the font is deleted.

Sample Programs

The following sample programs illustrate how these commands work.

Delete All Fonts

This program deletes all downloaded fonts, including those designated as permanent when downloaded. It also removes font number assignments from internal and cartridge fonts.

```
E$ = CHR$(27)          ' ESCAPE CHARACTER
LPRINT E$;"*c0F"       ' DELETE ALL FONTS
END
```

Delete Temporary Fonts

This program deletes all downloaded fonts designated as "temporary" when they were downloaded.

```
E$ = CHR$(27)          ' ESCAPE CHARACTER
LPRINT E$;"*c1F"       ' DELETE TEMPORARY FONTS
END
```

Delete Font by ID Number

This program deletes the font that has a font ID number of 1.

```
E$ = CHR$(27)          ' ESCAPE CHARACTER
LPRINT E$;"(1X";       ' SELECT FONT 1
LPRINT E$;"*c2F"       ' DELETE FONT WITH MOST
                       ' RECENTLY SPECIFIED
                       ' FONT ID NUMBER, IN
                       ' THIS CASE 1.
END
```

Delete Most Recent Download Character

This program shows how you can use this command to delete the last character sent to the printer in any downloaded font.

```
E$ = CHR$(27)              ' ESCAPE CHARACTER

LPRINT E$;"(15X";          ' SELECT FONT 15 AS
                           '   PRIMARY FONT
LPRINT E$;"*c3F"           ' DELETE MOST RECENTLY
                           ' DOWNLOADED CHARACTER
                           ' IN THE  MOST RECENTLY
                           ' SPECIFIED FONT, IN
                           ' THIS CASE, FONT 15
END
```

You could use this program to easily add a special character as the last character to a commercially available font. For example, in a USASCII font, the last character is the tilde (~), which is not used often in English. You might, however, find the registered trademark symbol (®) more useful. Use this program to delete the tilde from the font; then, separately download the trademark symbol. See the next chapter for details on how to download fonts.

Make a Font Temporary

This program makes font 25 temporary, regardless of what it was previously. Temporary fonts are erased by the reset command, ESC E.

```
E$ = CHR$(27)                    ' ESCAPE CHARACTER

LPRINT E$;"(25X";                ' SELECT FONT 25
LPRINT E$;"*c4F"                 ' MAKE FONT WITH MOST
                                 ' RECENTLY
                                 ' SPECIFIED FONT ID
                                 ' NUMBER TEMPORARY

END
```

Make a Font Permanent

This program makes font 35 permanent, regardless of what it was previously. Permanent fonts *are not* erased by the reset command, <u>ESC</u> E.

```
E$ = CHR$(27)                      ' ESCAPE CHARACTER

LPRINT E$;"(35X";                  ' SELECT FONT 35
LPRINT E$;"*c5F"                   ' MAKE FONT WITH MOST
                                   ' RECENTLY SPECIFIED
                                   ' FONT ID NUMBER
                                   ' TEMPORARY
END
```

Assigning a Font ID Number

This program assigns a font ID number to the current font:

```
E$ = CHR$(27)                      ' ESCAPE CHARACTER

' SELECT PRIMARY FONT
---------------------
LPRINT E$;"(8U";                   ' ROMAN-8 SYMBOL SET
LPRINT E$;"(s1p10v0s0b5T";         ' 10 PT TIMES ROMAN

LPRINT CHR$(15);                   ' SI TO ENSURE CURRENT
                                   ' FONT IS PRIMARY FONT

LPRINT E$;"*c45D";                 ' SET CURRENT FONT ID
                                   ' NUMBER AS 45

LPRINT E$;"*c6F";                  ' ASSIGN CURRENT FONT ID
                                   ' NUMBER (45) TO THE
                                   ' CURRENT FONT, THE 10
                                   ' PT ROMAN PRIMARY FONT
                                   ' WE ALREADY SPECIFIED.
END
```

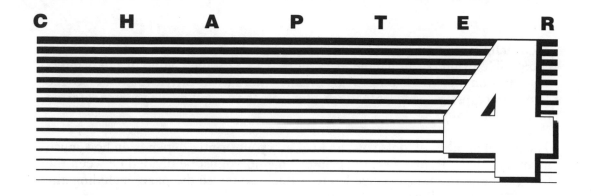

DOWNLOADING FONTS

A LaserJet + can accomodate up to 32 fonts in its font pool at any one time. Some compatible printers can handle even more than 32 fonts. None of the printers currently on the market have that many internal or cartridge fonts, so the remainder must be loaded into the printer from the computer — a process referred to as **downloading**.

The actual number of fonts you can load into your printer depends on how much memory it has. Remember, the printer's memory must be divided between the font pool and the memory needed to actually compose the page, including any raster (bit-mapped) graphics (see Chapter 9).

Some LaserJet + compatible printers partition memory, setting aside part of it for fonts and another part for raster graphics. See your printer documentation for the details on how your particular printer divides its memory.

HOW TO DOWNLOAD FONTS

Five steps are required to download a font:

1. Assign a **font ID** number.

2. Download the **font descriptor**.

3. Specify each **character** to download.

4. Give the **character descriptor** and **bit map** for each character.

5. After you have downloaded all the characters, designate the font as either **permanent** or **temporary**.

If you are downloading an entire font, perform steps 1, 4, and 5 *once* for each font; however, you must *repeat* steps 2 and 3 for each character.

ARGUMENTS

Arguments are numbers in a command that tell the printer "how many." For example, in the command to set the page length to 65 lines,

ESC &l 65 F

65 is the argument. It tells the printer to set the line spacing at 65 lines.

In most LaserJet+ commands in this book, the argument is represented by the symbol #, so the command to set page length is

ESC &l 65 F

Also, in most LaserJet+ commands, the argument is in ASCII printable characters. This means that to tell the printer to set the page length to 65 lines, you send the argument as the characters that normally print as 6 and 5.

However, in many font downloading commands in this chapter, arguments must be in a form the printer can understand directly as a number. To understand this difference, you must understand something about the internal workings of computers and printers.

Inside the computer (and printer) *everything* is a number. When you press the A key on your keyboard, the keyboard actually produces a number. For the letter A, that number happens to be 65. However, the computer knows that you are expecting a letter, so it looks up a pattern of dots in its memory that looks like the letter A and prints those dots on the screen. When you send the number 65 to a printer, the printer knows that most of the time you want it to print the letter A, and it does so.

The American Standard Code for Information Interchange (ASCII) specifies which letters, digits, and punctuation marks correspond to each number. Appendix C contains a listing of the ASCII code. If you examine this listing, you can see that the decimal number 65 corresponds to the letter A, 66 to the letter B, 112 to the letter p, 33 to the character !, and so on. When you press any of those keys, you are actually creating the corresponding number inside the computer.

When an argument is in ASCII form, it consists of the printable numbers that make up the value. So, for example, to specify a page length of 65 lines, you would send the printer the following sequence of characters:

<u>ESC</u> &1 65 F

The 6 and 5 (actually 54 and 53 inside the computer and printer) would specify that you wanted 65 lines.

However, if you were designing a printer, you could also choose to use the letter A to stand for 65 because, inside a computer and between computers and printers, A actually *is* the number 65. When you use A for 65, B for 66, p for 112, and ! for 33, and so on, you are using **decimal** arguments.

Many of the font download commands in this chapter use a mix of ASCII arguments and decimal arguments. Make sure you are using the right kind of argument in each command.

When there might be confusion in commands, a subscript D (as in 65_D) indicates decimal data; a subscript A (as in A_A) indicates ASCII data.

STEP 1—ASSIGN A FONT ID NUMBER

The following command assigns the font ID number # to the font you are about to download.

<u>Command</u>   <u>Explanation</u>

<u>ESC</u> *c # D   # is an ASCII number between 0 and 32767.

STEP 2—DOWNLOAD THE
FONT DESCRIPTOR (FONT HEADER)

The first item you send to the printer when preparing to download the font is the font descriptor or font header — information that describes the font. Later, when you select a font by description, the printer looks for the information in the font header to match a font to your request.

Command	Explanation
<u>ESC</u>) s # W {header data}	# is the number of bytes in the descriptor data, almost always 26. # is in ASCII form rather than decimal, so it is the characters 2 and 6.

The Header Data

The font header data is a series of bytes that describe the characteristics of a font. Send this data to the printer *once* for each font you are downloading.

Each byte in the header data specifies a particular font characteristic. For example, the twelfth byte of header data specifies whether the font is portrait or landscape orientation. If it is a portrait font, that byte is 0_D. If it is a landscape font, that byte is 1_D.

There are almost always 26 bytes of header data. Several of the bytes in the header data are always 0_D and have no function.

The font header data must be in binary format, which means, for example, that to send the printer the value 65, you send the letter A. (See the previous discussion of arguments.)

Bytes 0 and 1—Length of Header Data

These bytes repeat the number of bytes in the header data; they will almost always be 0_D and 26_D. Theoretically, though, these two bytes could each be 255_D, specifying a header data sequence of up to 65,535 characters.

Byte 2

Always 0_D.

Byte 3—Font Type

0_D specifies a 7-bit font (only characters 33 through 127 are printable).

1_D specifies an 8-bit font (characters 33 through 127 and 160 through 255 are printable).

Bytes 4 and 5

Always O_D.

Bytes 6 and 7—Baseline Position

These two bytes give the baseline distance from the top of the cell. In Figure 4.1, this distance is 30 dots, so these two bytes would be 0_D and 30_D. The baseline must, of course, fall within the cell, so it may be any number between 0 and the cell height minus 1.

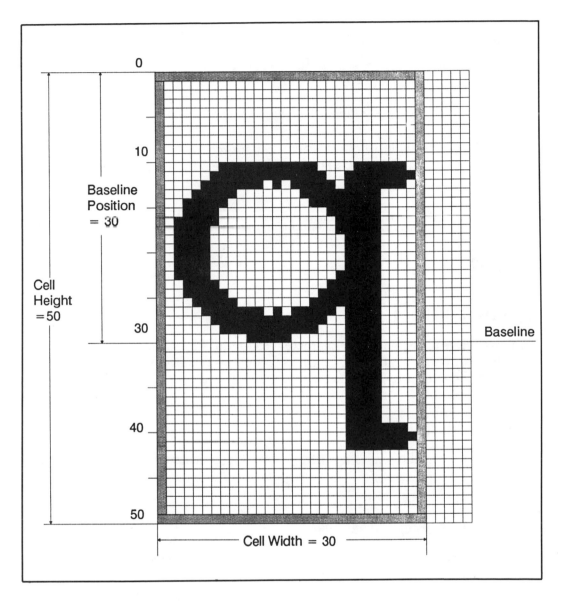

Figure 4.1   *Font Descriptors*

Byte 8

Always 0$_D$.

Byte 9—Cell Width

This byte gives the width of the character cell for the font. The width is measured in dots. In Figure 4.1, it is 30, so this byte would be 30$_D$. Cells may be up to 255 dots wide.

Byte 10

Always 0$_D$.

Byte 11—Cell Height

This byte gives the height of the character cell for this font. The height is measured in dots. In Figure 4.1, the cell height is 50 dots so this byte would be 50$_D$ (2$_A$). Cells may be from 1 to 255 dots high.

Byte 12—Orientation

0$_D$ indicates that the font is a portrait font. 1$_D$ indicates that it is a landscape font.

Byte 13—Fixed/Proportional Spacing

0$_D$ indicates that the font is a fixed-space font. 1$_D$ indicates that it is a proportionally spaced font.

Bytes 14 and 15—Symbol Set

These two bytes indicate which HP LaserJet+ symbol set the font uses. You compute the value of these bytes by taking the two characters of the symbol set designator (such as 0U for the USASCII character set) and dividing it into its two components — the leading number and the following letter. Look up the ASCII value of the uppercase version of the letter in the ASCII chart in Appendix C. Insert that value into the following formula:

(leading number × 32) + (ASCII value of letter) - 64

See Figure 2.2 (Chapter 2) for a list of some of the available symbol sets.

Examples of Symbol Set Computation

The following is how the formula works for the USASCII symbol set, 0U. The ASCII value of U is 85, so the formula is

(0 x 32) + 85 - 64 = 21

The symbol set bytes for the USASCII symbol set are 0D and 21D.

For the Roman-8 symbol set, the symbol set designator is 8U. The ASCII value of U is 85, so the formula is

(8 × 32) + 85 - 64 = (256) + 85 - 64 = 277

Because 277 is greater than 255, you cannot express it as a single byte. Remember, individual bytes can only run from 0 to 255. (See Appendices A and B for more information.) For this reason, you need one byte for the 256 and another for the balance.

When this value is greater than 255, use byte 14 to give the number of multiples of 256 and byte 15 for the balance. For example, for a value of 277, such as you get for a Roman-8 symbol set, divide 277 by 256, calculate the result to the decimal point and use it as byte 14, and then use the remainder as byte 15.

$$256\overline{)277} \quad \begin{array}{r} 1 \\ \underline{256} \\ 21 \end{array}$$

The values for these two bytes would be 1_D (representing a value of 256) and 21_D (the balance).

$$(1 \times 256) + 21 = 277$$

Bytes 16 and 17—Pitch (Default Horizontal Motion Index)

These two bytes specify the default pitch of the font, which is measured in dots and multiplied by 4.

For example, for a 10-pitch font, you must move 30 dots for each character because there are 10 characters per inch and 300 dots per inch. Multiply that value (30) by 4 to find the value to be inserted in this position, 120_D. For byte 16, send a 0_D to the printer, followed by 120_D for byte 17.

Another example is for 12-pitch type. To achieve 12 characters per inch at 300 dots per inch, you must advance 25 dots for each character ($300/12 = 25$). $25 \times 4 = 100$, so the value of byte 16 would again be 0_D, and the value of byte 17 would be 100_D.

The valid range for bytes 16 and 17 is from 2 to 1260. As with the previous values, when these values exceed 255, use byte 16 to give the number of multiples of 256, and use byte 17 for the balance. For example, for a value of 1156, divide 1156 by 256, calculate it to the decimal point for byte 16, and use the remainder for byte 17:

```
           4
    256)1156
        1024
         132
```

The value of byte 16, then, is 4D, and the value of byte 17 is 132D.

Because the value of these two bytes is four times the pitch, you can specify pitches accurately to within a quarter of a dot.

Bytes 18 and 19—Height

These two bytes specify the height of the font, which is different from the cell height; the cell height includes the distance between lines and is the same as the default line spacing for the font. Font height is measured in dots and multiplied by 4. For a font that is 50 dots high (6 lines per inch), use a value of 200D (50 × 4). The valid range is from 0 to 10922.

Bytes 20, 21, and 22

Always 0D.

Byte 23—Style (Upright or Italic)

Use 0D for an upright font, 1D for an italic font.

Byte 24—Stroke Weight (Boldness)

This byte specifies the font's boldness. 0_D is a normal-weight font. Bold fonts range from 1_D to 7_D. Lighter-than-normal stroke weights range from 249_D (-7) to 255_D (-1).

Byte 25—Typeface

This byte specifies the typeface. The following chart shows the values of byte 25 that have been standardized by Hewlett-Packard.

(See Figure 4.2 on next page)

Value or #	Typeface
0D	Line Printer
1D	Pica
2D	Elite
3D	Courier
4D	HELV (Helvetica, Swiss)
5D	TMS RMN (Times Roman, Dutch)
6D	Gothic
7D	Script
8D	Prestige
9D	Caslon
10D	Orator
11D	Presentation
12D	Helvetica Condensed
14D	Futura
15D	Palatino (Zapf Calligraphic)
16D	Souvenir
17D	Zapf Humanist (Optima)
18D	Garamond
19D	Cooper
20D	Coronet
21D	Broadway
22D	Bodoni
23D	Century Schoolbook
24D	University Roman
25D	Avant Garde Gothic
27D	Korinna
28D	Bitstream Charter
29D	Cloister Black
30D	Galliard
136D	Futura Book
146D	Futura Light
148D	Helvetica Light

Figure 4.2   *Standardized Hewlett-Packard Values for Byte 25*

STEP 3—CHARACTER IDENTIFICATION

This command must be sent to the printer once for each character you want to download.

Command	Explanation
ESC *c # E	# is the ASCII number of the character that will be downloaded next. It is a 1-, 2-, or 3-digit ASCII number between 0 and 255.

For example, if you are downloading a character to be printed in place of A, # will be the characters 6 and 5 because 65 is the ASCII number of the letter A. So the complete sequence will be as follows:

ESC *c 65 E

STEP 4—CHARACTER DESCRIPTOR AND DATA

The following command must be sent to the printer immediately after the character identification command. It describes the character you want to download and then provides a bit map showing where each dot goes.

Command	Explanation
ESC (s # W {character data}	# is the number of bytes (in ASCII form) that will be used to describe and bit map the character. The character data are 16 bytes of description followed by the bit map of the character. The curly brackets are not sent to the printer.

The Character Description Data

There are 16 bytes of description that precede the character bit map. All the bytes in the character descriptor are decimal. The 16 bytes of the character descriptor are as follows:

Byte 0

Always 4$_D$.

Byte 1

Always 0$_D$.

Byte 2

Always 14$_D$.

Byte 3

Always 1$_D$.

Byte 4—Orientation

This byte describes the orientation of the character. 0$_D$ describes portrait orientation. 1$_D$ describes landscape orientation.

Byte 5

Always 0$_D$.

Bytes 6 and 7—Left Offset

Left offset is the distance in dots from the character reference point (the position where the last printed letter left the print position) to the left edge of the character. The left offset is a number between -128 and 127. A 0_D in byte 6 indicates that the value in byte 7 is positive. A 1_D in byte 6 indicates that the value in byte 7 is negative.

Examine the landscape character in Figure 4.3. Note that because a landscape character is actually lying on its left side, the left offset value is -20; the distance from the character reference point to the left side of the character is 20 dots to the left. So the values in bytes 6 and 7 of the character descriptor string would be 1_D and 20_D.

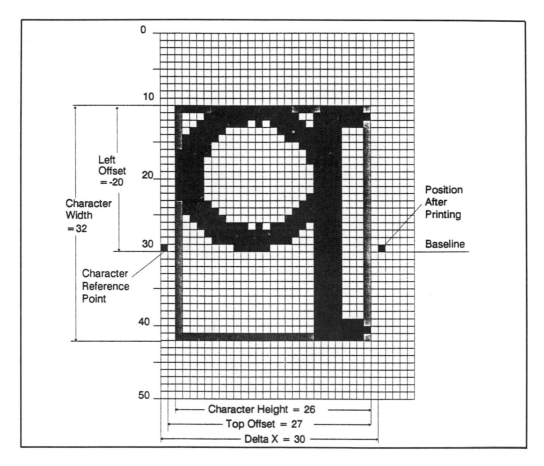

Figure 4.3   Landscape Character

In the portrait character in Figure 4.4, the left offset is 2, so the values in bytes 6 and 7 would be 0$_D$ and 2$_D$, respectively.

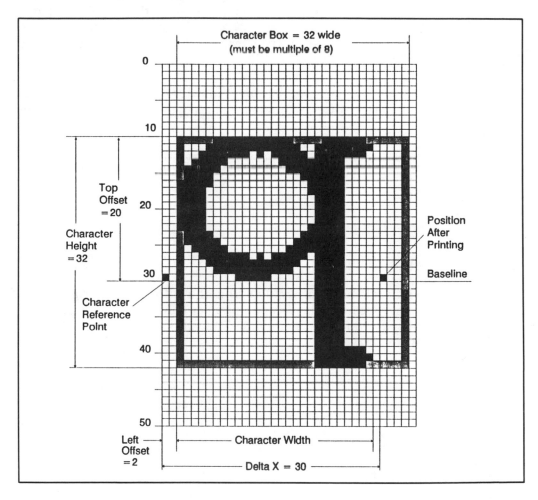

Figure 4.4   *Portrait Character*

Bytes 8 and 9—Top Offset

The **top offset** is the distance in dots from the character reference point (the position where the last printed letter left the print position) to the top of the character. The top offset is a number between -127 and 127. A 0_D in byte 8 indicates that the value in byte 9 is positive. A 1_D in byte 8 indicates that the value in byte 9 is negative.

In Figure 4.3, the top offset is 27, so the values in bytes 8 and 9 would be 0_D and 27_D. In Figure 4.4, the top offset is 20, so the values in bytes 8 and 9 would be 0_D and 20_D.

Byte 10

Always 0_D.

Byte 11—Character Width

The **character width** is the distance in dots from the left side to the right side of a portrait character. Because a landscape character is lying on its side, its width is its apparent height. Refer to Figure 4.3. The valid values for the character width byte are 0_D to 128_D.

Byte 12

Always 0_D.

Byte 13—Character Height

The **character height** is the distance in dots from the top to the bottom of a portrait character. Because a landscape character is lying on its side, its height is its apparent width. Refer to Figure 4.3. The valid values for the character height byte are 0_D to 128_D.

Bytes 14 and 15—Delta X

Delta x is the distance the print position travels after printing the character. Delta x is measured in dots and multiplied by 4. In Figures 4.3 and 4.4, it is the distance between the character reference point and the position after printing. Delta x is only used for proportionally spaced fonts.

Because the printer will not accept fractional values, the delta x bytes must always be multiples of four. For example, if you want the print position to move 30 dots, the value of the delta x bytes will be 0_D and 120_D.

Bytes 16 and On—Character Bit Map

Character bit maps describe patterns of dots that comprise characters. The bit maps read across the width of the character, starting in the upper left corner. If there is a dot in a location, the value of the bit that represents that location is 1. If there is no dot, the value is 0. Each group of eight bits makes up a byte.

For example, in Figure 4.4 there are no dots in the first five locations, but there are dots in the next three, which makes a byte of

00000111

The value of this byte is 7_D (ones in the 4s, 2s, and 1s columns), so the first byte of the character bit map is 7_D.

The second byte is

11111111

or 255_D (ones in the 128s, 64s, 32s, 16s, 8s, 4s, 2s, and 1s columns).

The third byte is

00001111

or 15D (ones in the 8s, 4s, 2s, and 1s columns)·

The last byte in the first row is

10000000

or 128D (a one in the 128s column).

Bit Maps for Landscape Characters

For landscape characters, because they are (in a sense) lying on their left sides, the bit map starts at the upper right corner and moves down and to the left.

STEP 5—MAKE FONT TEMPORARY/PERMANENT

These commands designate a downloaded font as temporary (erased by the reset command, ESC E) or permanent (not erased by the reset command).

Command	Explanation
ESC *c 4F	Temporary
ESC *c 5 F	Permanent

Sample Font Download

The following program combines the concepts you have just learned to create a special font to print a single character – a small maple leaf.

You could also print this logo, using a raster graphics program as explained in Chapter 9; however, if you use a particular visual image often, as you would a logo, it is a better idea to store it as a macro (see Chapter 11) or a font character, which allows you to use the image more quickly and easily.

```
' ============= MAPLE.BAS ===============
'
' THIS PROGRAM CREATES A LASERJET+ FONT
' CONTAINING ONE CHARACTER: A MAPLE LEAF
' LOGO
'
' YOU CAN EASILY ADAPT IT TO CREATE ANY FONT
' WITH ANY NUMBER OF CHARACTERS
'
' =====================================

' --- PRELIMINARIES ---

' DECLARE SUBPROGRAMS AND FUNCTIONS
  DECLARE SUB LoadCharacter (E$)
  DECLARE FUNCTION ConvertBinary% (DATA2$)

  E$ = CHR$(27)                    ' ESCAPE CHARACTER
  FF$ = CHR$(12)                   ' FORM FEED CHARACTER
  LF$ = CHR$(10)                   ' LINE FEED CHARACTER

' --- SETUP PRINTER ---
  OPEN "LPT1:" FOR OUTPUT AS #1    ' OPEN PRINTER AS FILE
  WIDTH "LPT1:", 255               ' OVERRIDE AUTO CR/LF
  PRINT #1, E$; "E";               ' RESET

' ASSIGN FONT ID NUMBER - FONT 100
  PRINT #1, E$; "*c100D";
```

continued...

...from previous page

```
' --- DOWNLOAD FONT DESCRIPTOR (HEADER) ---

  PRINT #1, E$; ")s26W";              ' START FONT HEADER
  PRINT #1, CHR$(0); CHR$(26);        ' 0/1 - LENGTH OF
                                      ' DESCRIPTOR DATA
  PRINT #1, CHR$(0);                  ' 2 - ALWAYS 0
  PRINT #1, CHR$(0);                  ' 3 - FONT TYPE -  7 BIT
  PRINT #1, CHR$(0); CHR$(0);         ' 4/5 - ALWAYS 0
  PRINT #1, CHR$(0); CHR$(30);        ' 6/7 - BASELINE POS.
  PRINT #1, CHR$(0);                  ' 8 - ALWAYS 0
  PRINT #1, CHR$(48);                 ' 9 - CELL WIDTH
  PRINT #1, CHR$(0);                  ' 10 - ALWAYS 0
  PRINT #1, CHR$(50);                 ' 11 - CELL HEIGHT
  PRINT #1, CHR$(0);                  ' 12 - PORTRAIT ORIENT.
  PRINT #1, CHR$(1);                  ' 13 - PROPORTIONAL
                                      ' SPACING
  PRINT #1, CHR$(1); CHR$(241);       ' 14/15 - SYMBOL SET 15Q
  PRINT #1, CHR$(0); CHR$(192);       ' 16/17 - PITCH 48 DOTS
  PRINT #1, CHR$(0); CHR$(200);       ' 18/19 - HEIGHT 50 DOTS
  PRINT #1, CHR$(0); CHR$(0);         ' 20/21 -  ALWAYS 0
  PRINT #1, CHR$(0);                  ' 22 - ALWAYS 0
  PRINT #1, CHR$(0);                  ' 23 - UPRIGHT STYLE
  PRINT #1, CHR$(0);                  ' 24 - NORMAL WEIGHT
  PRINT #1, CHR$(0);                  ' 25 - LINE PRINTER
                                      ' TYPEFACE

' --- SPECIFY THE CHARACTER ---
  PRINT #1, E$; "*c126E";             ' REPLACE TILDE (~)
```

continued...

...from previous page

```
' --- DOWNLOAD THE CHARACTER DESCRIPTOR ---

    PRINT #1, E$; "(s161W";            ' START SEQUENCE
                                       ' 161 CHARACTERS
                                       ' LONG: 16
                                       ' DESCRIPTOR PLUS
                                       ' 145 BIT MAP (29
                                       ' ROWS OF 5 BYTES
                                       ' EACH)
    PRINT #1, CHR$(4);                 ' 0 - ALWAYS 4
    PRINT #1, CHR$(0);                 ' 1 - ALWAYS 0
    PRINT #1, CHR$(14);                ' 2 - ALWAYS 14
    PRINT #1, CHR$(1);                 ' 3 - ALWAYS 1
    PRINT #1, CHR$(0);                 ' 4 - ORIENTATION
    PRINT #1, CHR$(0);                 ' 5 - ALWAYS 0
    PRINT #1, CHR$(0); CHR$(2);        ' 6/7 - LEFT OFFSET
    PRINT #1, CHR$(0); CHR$(28);       ' 8/9 - TOP OFFSET
    PRINT #1, CHR$(0); CHR$(40);       ' 10/11 - WIDTH
    PRINT #1, CHR$(0); CHR$(29);       ' 12/13 - HEIGHT
    PRINT #1, CHR$(0); CHR$(192);      ' 14/15 - DELTA X

' --- DOWNLOAD THE BIT MAP ---
    CALL LoadCharacter(E$)             ' THIS LOADS THE
                                       ' CHARACTER BIT MAP

' --- SET AS TEMPORARY FONT ---
    PRINT #1, E$; "*c4F";

' --- SELECT INTERNAL COURIER FONT AND PRINT SOMETHING ---
    PRINT #1, E$; "(8U"; E$; "(s0p12v10h0s0b1T";
    PRINT #1, "Hello from the land of the Maple Leaves ";

' -- SELECT THE NEW FONT ---
    PRINT #1, E$; "(100X";
```

continued...

...from previous page

```
' --- PRINT THE CHARACTER ---
  PRINT #1, "˜";

' --- SWITCH BACK AND PRINT SOME MORE ---
  PRINT #1, E$; "(8U"; E$; "(s0p12v10h0s0b1T";
  PRINT #1, " See what I mean?"

PRINT #1, FF$                       ' EJECT PAGE
CLOSE #1                            ' CLOSE FILE (PRINTER)


' ---------------------------------------------------
'
' THESE DATA LINES CONTAIN THE ACTUAL DATA FOR
' THE PICTURE.  # MEANS A DOT IN THAT LOCATION.
' ANYTHING ELSE MEANS NO DOT
'
' EACH LINE OF DATA MUST CONTAIN A NUMBER OF CHARACTERS THAT
' IS AN EXACT MULTIPLE OF EIGHT.
'
' THE LAST LINE OF THE DATA MUST READ "END OF DATA".
'
' ---------------------------------------------------
```

continued...

...from previous page

```
'       |    1   |    2   |    3   |    4   |    5
DATA   |'''''''|'''''''|''#''''|'''''''|'''''''
DATA   |''''''''|''''''#'|'###'''#'|'''''''|'''''''
DATA   |-------|-----##|#####-##-------|-------
DATA   |'''''''|''''''#####'#####'''''''|'''''''
DATA   |'''''''#'''|''####'''####''''#'|'''''''
DATA   |''''''##''|'###''''###''''##'|'''''''
DATA   |'''''''###'''|'###''''###'''###'|'''''''
DATA   |'-------####--###-----###--####-|-------
DATA   |'''########'###''''###'########'''''
DATA   |'''###########'''''###########'''''
DATA   |'''###'|'######''''######'''###'''''
DATA   |'''###'|'######''''######'''###'''''
DATA ######-|----####-----####-------######-
DATA   |#####''|''''###''''###''''''|#####''
DATA   |'#####'|''''##''''##'|'''''#####'''
DATA   |''#####|''''''#''''#'|''''''#####'''
DATA   |''#####''''''''|'''''''|'''''#####'''''
DATA   |'---#####-------|-------|----#####------
DATA   |'''''#####'''''|'''''''|'''#####''''''
DATA   |''''''#####''''|'''''''|''#####|'''''''
DATA   |''''''''######''|'''''''|'#####'|'''''''
DATA   |'''''''|######'|'''''''|#####''|'''''''
DATA   |'-------|-#################---|-------
DATA   |'''''''|''################''''|'''''''
DATA   |'''''''|'''##############'''''|'''''''
DATA   |'''''''|'''''''|#####''|'''''''|'''''''
DATA   |'''''''|'''''''|#####''|'''''''|'''''''
DATA   |-------|-------|#####--|-------|-------
DATA   |'''''''|'''''''|#####''|'''''''|'''''''
DATA END OF DATA
```

continued...

81

...from previous page

```
' ------------ConvertBinary%---------------
'
' THIS FUNCTION CONVERTS A STRING CONTAINING
' # CHARACTERS INTO A DECIMAL NUMBER.  A # IN
' ANY POSITION MEANS THE VALUE OF THAT POSITION
' IS A 1.  ANYTHING ELSE IS A 0.
'
' ------------------------------------------
'
FUNCTION ConvertBinary% (DATA2$)

  BinVALUE% = 0
  BINARYCOUNTER% = 1

  FOR Z% = 8 TO 1 STEP -1
     IF MID$(DATA2$, Z%, 1) = "#" THEN
     ' ADD VALUE OF PLACE
       BinVALUE% = BinVALUE% + BINARYCOUNTER%
     END IF
  BINARYCOUNTER% = BINARYCOUNTER% * 2   ' INCREMENT BINARY
                                        ' PLACE VALUE
  NEXT Z%
  ConvertBinary% = BinVALUE%

END FUNCTION
'
' -------------- LoadCharacter --------------
'
' THIS SUBPROGRAM ACTUALLY LOADS THE CHARACTER BITMAP
'
' ------------------------------------------
'
SUB LoadCharacter (E$) STATIC
```

continued...

...from previous page

```
DO WHILE DATA$ <> "END OF DATA"       ' STOPS AT END OF
                                      ' CHARACTER

  READ DATA$                          ' READ ONE LINE OF
                                      ' DOT PATTERNS FROM
                                      ' DATA STATEMENTS
  FOR Y% = 1 TO 40 STEP 8             ' CELL WIDTH = 40
    DATA2$ = MID$(DATA$, Y%, 8)       ' TAKE 8 CHARACTERS
    DATATOPRINT% = ConvertBinary%(DATA2$)      ' CONVERT TO
                                               ' DECIMAL NUMBER

    PRINT #1, CHR$(DATATOPRINT%);     ' SEND TO PRINTER
  NEXT Y%

LOOP

END SUB
```

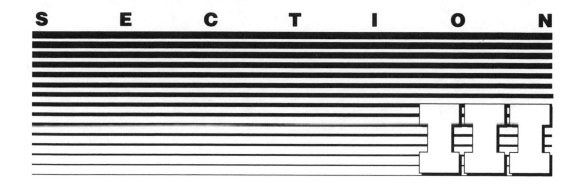

S E C T I O N

III

MOVING AROUND THE PAGE

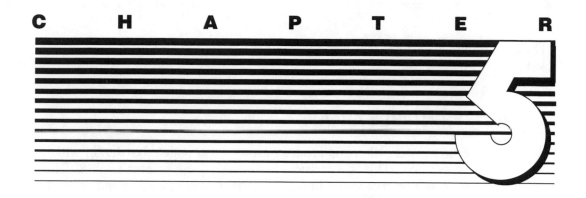

DIRECT PRINT POSITION CONTROL

The commands in this chapter directly move the print position to wherever you want it on the page.

THE NON-PRINTABLE AREA

With most laser printers, there is an area around the page's border in which nothing can be printed. This is a physical limitation of the printer engine. The size of the non-printable area varies depending on the printer engine, but on most machines, it is about 1/4" wide.

On most printers, you can issue commands to print in this area or to set the margins so that printing will normally fall in this area. The printers will accept these commands and dutifully—but unsuccessfully—try to print in the non-printable area.

PUSH/POP CURRENT PRINT POSITION

Use the following command when moving the print position around the page if you know you must return to a previous position.

Command	Explanation
ESC & f 0 S	Push (Save) current print position
ESC & f 1 S	Pop (Restore) last pushed print position

You can save up to 32 print positions in the MT910's memory with this command. The Pop command always moves the print position back to the most recently Pushed (saved) position.

CONTROLLING THE PRINT POSITION BY DOTS

Command	Explanation
ESC *p # X	Move print position # dots horizontally
ESC *p # Y #	Move print position # dots vertically

is the distance you want to move the print position, measured in dots (300 dots per inch).

If the value of # is preceded by a plus sign (+) or minus sign (-), the move is relative to the current print position. Positive values move the print position to the right or down. Negative values move the print position to the left or up.

If no sign precedes the #, the move is relative to the origin (the upper left corner of the page). Remember, the origin moves when you change print orientation from portrait to landscape, or vice versa.

This command can be used to move the print position outside the left, right, or bottom margins. The command does not, however, allow you to move the print position into the top margin. If you try to move into the top margin, the currently active print position will be moved to the margin and no farther. If you move the print position off the bottom of the page, the page will be ejected, and the printing will continue on the next page.

CONTROLLING THE PRINT POSITION BY DECIPOINTS

Command	Explanation
ESC *a # H	Move print position # decipoints horizontally
ESC *a # V	Move print position # decipoints vertically

is the distance you want to move the print position, measured in decipoints (720 decipoints = 1"). You can specify decipoint values accurate to two decimal places.

If the value of # is preceded by a plus sign (+) or minus sign (-), the move is relative to the current print position. Positive values move the print positon to the right or down. Negative values move the print position to the left or up.

If no sign precedes #, the move is relative to the origin, (the upper left corner of the page). Remember, the origin moves when you change print orientation from portrait to landscape, or vice versa. For example, the command

ESC &a 720 x 1440 Y

moves the print position 1" (720 decipoints) to the right and 2" (1440 decipoints) down from the origin, while the command

ESC &a +720 x -1440 Y

moves the print position 1" to the right and 2" up from the current print position.

This command can be used to move the print position outside the left, right, or bottom margins. The command does not, however, allow you to move the print position into the top margin. If you try to move into the top margin, the currently active print position will be moved to the margin and no farther. If you move the print position off the bottom of the page, the page will be ejected, and the printing will continue on the next page.

CONTROLLING THE PRINT POSITION BY ROWS AND COLUMNS

Command	Explanation
ESC *a # C	Move print position # columns horizontally
ESC *a # R	Move print position # rows vertically

is the distance you want to move the print position, measured in columns (for horizontal movement) or rows (for vertical movement). The size of a column is based on the current pitch (for fixed-space fonts) or the current **SPACE** character width (for proportionally spaced fonts). The size of a row is based on the current vertical line spacing.

You can specify moves in fractional rows or columns accurate to two decimal places. If the value # is preceded by a plus sign (+) or minus sign (-), the move is relative to the current print position. Positive values move the print position to the right or down. Negative values move the print position to the left or up.

If no sign precedes #, the move is relative to the origin (the upper left corner of the page). Remember, the origin moves when you change print orientation from portrait to landscape, or vice versa.

This command can be used to move the print position outside the left, right, or bottom margins. The command does not, however, allow you to move the print position into the top margin. If you try to move into the top margin, the currently active print position will be moved to the margin and no farther. If you move the print position off the bottom of the page, the page will be ejected, and the printing will continue on the next page.

For example,

ESC &a 10 c 12 R

moves the print position 1" (10 spaces) to the right and 2" (12 lines) down from the origin at the default character pitch and line spacing, while

ESC &a +10 c −12 R

moves the print position 1" (10 spaces) to the right and 2" (12 lines) up from the current print position at the default character pitch and line spacing.

SAMPLE PRINT POSITION MOVEMENT PROGRAM

This program first moves the print position 1" (300 dots) to the right and 2" (600 dots) down from the origin; then, it returns to the same starting position and moves 1" right and 2" down from the print position.

```
' ================== PRINTPOS.BAS =====================
'
' THIS PROGRAM JUST DEMONSTRATES THE LASERJET+ CURSOR
' MOVEMENT COMMANDS.
'
' ========================================================

E$ = CHR$(27)                        ' ESCAPE CHARACTER
BS$ = CHR$(8)                        ' BACKSPACE
FF$ = CHR$(12)                       ' FORM FEED

' MARK ORIGIN
  LPRINT "v"; BS$; "| Origin is here."

' SET STARTING POINT BY SPACING DOWN 30 LINES
' AND RIGHT 1O SPACES

' SPACE DOWN 10 LINES
    FOR X = 1 TO 30: LPRINT : NEXT

' AND TO THE RIGHT 10 SPACES
    LPRINT "          ";

' MARK STARTING PRINT POSITION
    LPRINT "Relative move starts here v"; BS$; "|";

' SAVE CURRENT PRINT POSITION
    LPRINT E$; "&f0S";

' MOVE PRINT POSITION RELATIVE TO ORIGIN
    LPRINT E$; "*p300x";             ' MOVE 300 DOTS RIGHT
    LPRINT "600Y";                   ' AND 600 DOTS DOWN FROM
                                     ' ORIGIN

' MARK LOCATION AFTER MOVE
    LPRINT "v"; BS$; "| Origin move finishes here"

' RESTORE STARTING PRINT POSITION
    LPRINT E$; "&f1S";
```

continued...

...from previous page

```
' MOVE PRINT POSITION RELATIVE TO CURRENT POSITION
    LPRINT E$; "*p+300x";          ' MOVE 300 DOTS RIGHT
    LPRINT "+600Y";                ' AND 600 DOTS DOWN FROM
                                   ' CURRENT PRINT POSITION

' MARK LOCATION AFTER MOVE
    LPRINT "v"; BS$; "| Relative move finishes here"

LPRINT CHR$(12) ' FORM FEED TO EXPEL PAGE

END
```

Run the program. Note how the first part of the program measures the move from the origin at the upper left corner of the page, while the second part measures the move from the starting print position.

Try the same program, but vary it to move the print position by decipoints or rows and columns. See how the results vary.

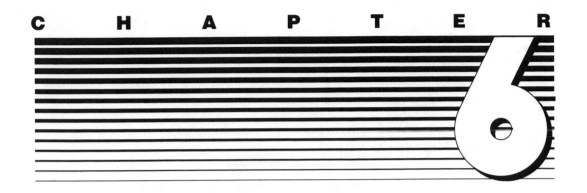

VERTICAL MOTION

Vertical motion commands control vertical aspects of the page, such as moving the print position up and down the page one line (or fraction of a line) at a time. See Chapter 5 for instructions on commands you can use to directly move the print position to any position on the page.

THE NON-PRINTABLE AREA

As mentioned in Chapter 5, with most laser printers there is an area around the page's border in which nothing can be printed. This is a physical limitation of the printer engine. The size of the non-printable area varies depending on the printer engine, but, on most printers, it is about 1/4" inch wide.

On most printers, you can issue commands to print in this area or set the margins so that printing will normally fall in this area. The printers will accept these commands and dutifully—but unsuccessfully—try to print in the non-printable area.

ADVANCING THE PRINT POSITION

The following commands move the print position up and down the page.

Line Feed

Command	Explanation
LF	Line feed

This command moves the print position down the page to the next line.

Set the line height with the Vertical Motion Index command, ESC &l # C, discussed later in this chapter or the Lines Per Inch command, ESC &l # D, also discussed later in this chapter.

Normally, LF will not move the print position back to the left margin unless the printer has been adjusted using the Line Termination command — ESC &k 2 G or ESC &k 3 G (see Chapter 7).

Reverse Line Feed

Command	Explanation
ESC &a −1 R	Reverse Line Feed

This command will move the print position up one line, based on the current line height.

Half-Line Feed

Command	Explanation
ESC =	Half-Line Feed

This command moves the print position down the page a distance equal to 1/2 the current line height.

Reverse Half-Line Feed

Command	Explanation
ESC &a −.5 R	Reverse Half-Line Feed

This command will move the print position up the page a distance equal to 1/2 the current line height.

Form Feed

Command	Explanation
FF	Form Feed

This command will move the print position up the page a distance equal to half the current line height.

You can also finish printing a page and eject it from the printer by moving the print position off the bottom of the page, using either the direct print position movement commands (see Chapter 5) or the command ESC &1 0 H.

LINE SPACING

Use the following commands to set the line spacing.

Set Vertical Motion Index

Command	Explanation
<u>ESC</u> &l # C	# is the line spacing in 1/48 " increments

The Vertical Motion Index (VMI) is the distance the print position moves down the page when the printer receives a Line Feed command.

The valid range for # is from 0 to 126, and decimal fractions are acceptable up to four places to the right of the decimal point.

For example, use the command <u>ESC</u> &l 6 C to set the line spacing to eight lines per inch. A line move of 6/48" is 1/8" or eight lines per inch. The following program performs that task:

```
E$ = CHR$(27)              ' ESCAPE CHARACTER
LPRINT E$;"&l6C";          ' SET LINE SPACING AT
                           ' 1/8 INCH

END
```

Set Line Spacing

Command	Explanation
ESC &l # D	# is the line spacing in lines per inch. # must be 1, 2, 3, 4, 6, 8, 12, 16, 24, or 48.

This command sets the line spacing in lines per inch.

For example, the command ESC &l 6 D sets the line spacing to six lines per inch. ESC &l 8 D sets it to eight lines per inch. If you send a # value that is not on the above list, this command is ignored.

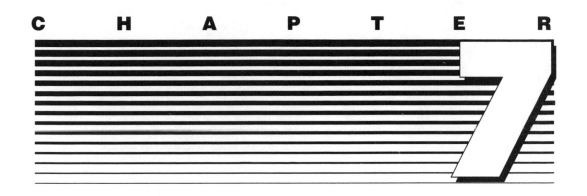

HORIZONTAL MOTION

The following commands control the horizontal motion of the print position.

BACKSPACE

Command	Explanation
BS	Backspace

This control code moves the current print position to the left by one column.

The most common use of the BS command is to create special print effects. For example, if you need the symbol for the Japanese Yen, ¥, but the font you are using doesn't include that symbol, you can create it by sending Y, then BS, and then = to the printer.

The distance the print position moves back to the left depends on the current Horizontal Motion Index (HMI), which is explained later in this chapter. In a proportional font, that distance may not be the same as the width of the character you have just printed; thus, the second character you wanted to print on top of another may not line up correctly. To avoid this problem, use the HMI command to set the size of the intended backspace; then, before continuing, issue the backspace, using SI to reset the HMI to the default on the primary font.

CARRIAGE RETURN

Command	Explanation
CR	Carriage Return

This control code normally moves the current print position to the left margin on the current line. Its action can be adjusted, however, by the Line Termination command (discussed later in this chapter).

HORIZONTAL MOTION INDEX

Command	Explanation
ESC &k # H	# is the Horizontal Motion Index in 1/120" increments.

The valid range for # is from 0 to 126, with up to four places after the decimal point.

The **horizontal motion index** is the distance the print position advances along the line for each character (in a fixed-space font) or the distance the print positin advances when the printer receives the SPACE character (for a proportionally spaced font). It is also the distance the print position moves backwards for a BS command.

You can use this command to override the spacing of a font. With a proportionally spaced font, this will make the SPACE and BS characters the width you specify. In a fixed-space font, the entire font will have the spacing you specify, so, for example, you could do the following:

```
print a 10 pitch font at 14 pitch like this.
or  at  8  pitch  like  this.
```

The HMI returns to a font's default HMI (the width of the space character in that font) whenever you change the orientation, symbol set, pitch, proportional spacing, or height of a font or whenever you use the SI or SO commands to shift between the primary and secondary fonts.

DIRECT PRINT POSITION CONTROL WITH HMI

You can use the HMI command to move the print position to the right or left in 1/120" increments. First, set the HMI to 1/120"; then, use spaces or backspaces to move around.

For example, the following program moves the print position 1" to the right, using HMI:

```
E$ = CHR$(27)                          ' ESCAPE CHARACTER
LF$ = CHR$(10)                         ' LINE FEED CHARACTER
BS$ = CHR$(8)                          ' BACK SPACE CHARACTER

' SET HMI TO 1/120 INCH
  LPRINT E$;"&k1H";                    ' SET HMI

' MOVE 1 INCH TO THE RIGHT
  FOR X = 1 TO 120                     ' 120 SPACES AT 1/120
                    ' IN.
   LPRINT " ";
  NEXT X
' MARK IT
  LPRINT "*";                          ' JUST A MARKER

' MOVE DOWN ONE LINE
  LPRINT LF$;   ' LINE FEED

' MOVE 1/2 INCH TO THE LEFT
  FOR X = 1 TO 60
    LPRINT BS$;                        ' 60 BACKSPACES AT 1/120
                                       ' IN.

  NEXT X

' MARK IT
  LPRINT "+"                           ' JUST A MARKER

END
```

LINE TERMINATION

Command		#	CR	LF	FF
ESC &k # G	Explanation	#	CR	LF	FF
		0	CR	LF	FF
		1	CR + LF	LF	FF
		2	CR	CR+LF	CR+FF
		3	CR+LF	CR+LF	CR+FF

This command controls the action of the CR, LF, and FF commands. Depending on the value of #, the actions of these commands vary.

END-OF-LINE WRAP

Command	Explanation
ESC &s # C	# = 1 turns End-of-Line Wrap ON
	# = 0 turns End-of-Line Wrap OFF

When End-of-Line Wrap is turned ON and the printer receives a character that would normally print past the right margin, the printer executes a CR and LF command before printing the character at the beginning of the next line.

HORIZONTAL TABS

Command	Explanation
HT	Horizontal Tab

The Horizontal Tab command advances the print position to the next hardware tab stop. On the LaserJet Series II, hardware tabs are set every eight columns to the right of the left margin. On the LaserJet, LaserJet+, and LaserJet 500+, the horizontal tab character is ignored and has no effect. Do not use this command if you are programming to run on all LaserJets and compatibles. Instead, use the direct cursor positioning controls discussed in Chapter 5.

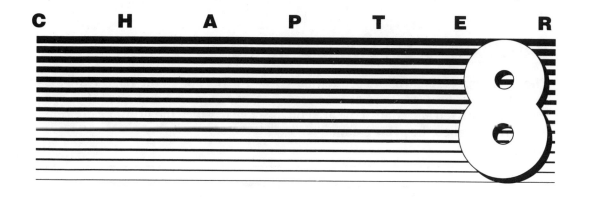

PAGE FORMATTING

HARDWARE vs. SOFTWARE MARGINS

These commands control the printer margins — the portion of the page available for printing. These are the hardware margins, which means that once they are set, they stay fixed and control the area on the page in which the printer can print. This area is called the **print column**.

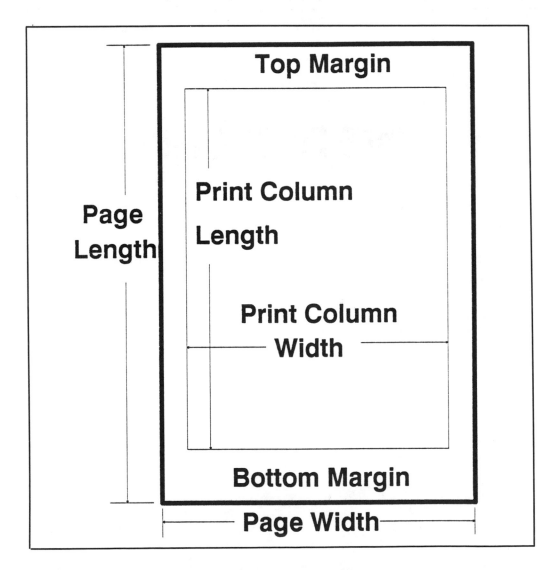

Figure 8.1   Page showing top, bottom, and side margins

Most computer programs do not use the hardware margins. Instead, they create margins by spacing down from the top with line feeds and in from the sides with spaces before printing. While this method is more flexible, you may occasionally want to program an application that can use hardware margin control.

THE NON-PRINTABLE AREA

As discussed previously, with most laser printers, there is an area around the page's border in which nothing can be printed. This is a physical limitation of the printer engine. The size of this area varies depending on the printer engine, but, on most printers, it is about 1/4" wide.

On most printers, you can issue commands to print in this area or to set the margins so that printing will normally fall in this area. The printers will accept these commands and dutifully — but unsuccessfully — try to print in the non-printable area.

SIDE MARGINS

Generally speaking, you cannot print in the side margins. The printer always starts printing a line at the left margin. If you attempt to print a line that extends into the right margin, the printer will automatically print the first character that exceeds the right margin back at the left margin. If the End-of-Line Wrap function is turned ON, that character will print on the next line; in other words, the printer will execute a carriage return and a line feed before printing that character. If the End-of-Line Wrap is left to the default or turned OFF, the printer will print that character on the same line the printer started on; in other words, it will execute a carriage return (but not a line feed) only before printing that character.

You can move the print position into the side margins, however, by using the direct print position control commands (see Chapter 5).

Set Side Margins

Command	Explanation
ESC &a # L	Set Left Margin
ESC &a # M	Set Right Margin

These commands set the left and right margins to column number #. The leftmost position on the page is column zero. If you try to set the left margin to the right of the right margin, the command is ignored.

The width of a column varies with the pitch of the current font. So, when you are using a 10-pitch font, column 10 is 1" to the right of the left edge of the paper. With a 12-pitch font, column 10 is only 5/6" (10/12") from the left edge. (Proportional fonts use the width of the **SPACE** character as the column width.)

Because column widths vary, it is a good idea to always set margins in the same font, preferably a fixed-space font, such as the resident Courier font. Then, using the Courier example, you know that each space represents 1/10". When you have set the margin, you can use whichever font you want.

Clear Side Margins

Command	Explanation
ESC 9	Clear Side Margins

This command clears the left and right margins and sets them back to the maximum printable width of the paper.

TOP AND BOTTOM MARGINS

As with the side margins, the printer will not normally allow you to print in the top or bottom margins.

You can use the direct print position control commands (Chapter 5) to move the print position into the bottom margin; however, if you accidentally move it too far and off the page, the printer will print the page.

You cannot move into the top margin — even with the direct print position commands.

Set Top Margin

Command	Explanation
ESC &l # E	Set a top margin of # lines

This command sets the top margin to # lines. The size of each line is set by the Line-spacing command (see Chapter 6). The range of values for # is from 0 to the page length.

The top margin is stored as an absolute value. Once you set it, you can change the vertical motion index (VMI) or line spacing without affecting the position of the top margin.

The printer will ignore this command if the command specifies a top margin off the bottom of the page or if the vertical motion index is set to zero.

The Top Margin and the Print Column

When you set the top margin, the print column length defaults to whatever length will produce a bottom margin of the same size. So if you set the top margin to 1", the print column length will default to 9" (assuming 11" paper), leaving a bottom margin of 1". If you want another print column length, follow the Set Top Margin command with a Set Page Length command to fool the printer into thinking it has paper of a different size loaded.

Set a New but Smaller Top Margin

You can set the top margin on a page at any time; however, if the print position is already below the new top margin, and you want to print at that new top margin, you must move the print position back to the top with a direct print position command, such as ESC &a 0 R, which moves the print position to row zero.

Note: Don't forget the non-printable area that is part of most laser printers. Don't use # values of 0 or 1, as they will cause the printer to move into this unprintable area, and you will lose several lines.

THE BOTTOM MARGIN

There is no command to set the bottom margin directly. The bottom margin is the page length minus the top margin and the print column length. Use these commands to set the various elements of the bottom margin.

The default bottom margin is 1/2".

There also is a non-printable area at the bottom of the page. Don't adjust your bottom margin to print in this position; you will probably lose several lines.

SET PAGE LENGTH

Command	Explanation
ESC &l # P	Set the page length to # lines, using the current line spacing

The page length is the physical length of the paper. The current line spacing is set by the most recent setting for the Line-spacing command (see Chapter 6).

Many LaserJet+ compatible printers can determine what size paper you are using from the paper cassette you have loaded. As a result, you will often not need this command. If, however, you are writing a commercial program that must run on a variety of printers, or if you want to use paper that is smaller than that for which the paper cassette was designed, use this command to inform the printer of the paper size you are using.

On most printers that can sense the paper length from the cassette, specifying a page length of 0 sets the page length to the length of the currently selected paper cassette.

On some printers, the default paper length for the manual feed slot differs based on the assumption that you wouldn't be hand-feeding paper if you were using a normal-sized sheet. For example, the page size may default to 14" (legal size).

Because of all these variations, if you are writing a program that will be run on a number of LaserJet+ compatibles, don't make any assumptions about paper length and margins. Specify everything as part of your program.

Page Length and Orientation

Remember, page length does not automatically change when you shift from portrait to landscape orientation. Be sure to specify the new page length before you switch orientation.

SET PRINT COLUMN LENGTH

Command	Explanation
ESC &l # F	Set the print column length to # lines

If you specify a print column length of 0, the printer ignores the command and sets the bottom margin to the default 1/2". If you attempt to set a print column length that forces the bottom margin off the page, the printer will ignore the command.

PERFORATION-SKIP MODE

Command	Explanation
ESC &l # L	# = 1 turns Perforation-Skip ON
	# = 0 turns Perforation-Skip OFF

When Perforation-Skip mode is OFF, the printer ignores the bottom margin. You might want to turn this mode off if you are controlling all your margins with software. Remember, however, that ignoring the bottom margin might move the print position into the non-printable area at the bottom of the page.

The name of this feature is derived from continuous-feed printer paper used in many dot matrix printers. Each page is attached to the next by perforations. The Perforation-Skip mode made sure the printer did not print on the tear line between sheets of paper.

AN EXAMPLE OF MARGIN SETTING

This program sets margins of 1" on top, 1" for the sides and bottom, and ensures that the Perforation-Skip feature is turned ON.

```
E$ = CHR$(27)                       ' ESCAPE CHARACTER

' TOP AND BOTTOM MARGINS
' ---------------------
' SET LINE SPACING

    LPRINT E$;"&l6D";               ' SET SPACING AT 6
                                    ' LINES/IN


' SET PAGE LENGTH - REMEMBER, PRESUME NOTHING

    LPRINT E$;"&l66P";              ' SET PAGE LENGTH AT 11
                                    ' INCHES (66 LINES)


' SET TOP MARGIN TO ONE INCH.  REMEMBER, THIS ALSO SETS
' THE BOTTOM MARGIN TO 1 INCH SO WE'LL HAVE TO ADJUST IT.

    LPRINT E$;"&l6E";               ' SET TOP MARGIN TO 1
                                    ' INCH (6 LINES)


' SET PRINT COLUMN LENGTH (AND BOTTOM MARGIN)
    LPRINT E$;"&l51F";              ' SET PRINT COLUMN
                                    ' LENGTH TO 51 LINES
                                    ' (8.5" @ 6 LINES/IN)
                                    ' LEAVING 1.5" FOR THE
                                    ' BOTTOM MARGIN (11"
                                    ' PAGE LENGTH LESS 1"
                                    ' TOP MARGIN AND 8.5"
                                    ' PRINT COLUMN LENGTH).
```

continued...

...from previous page

```
' SIDE MARGINS
' ------------

' SELECT FONT WITH KNOWN SPACING - INTERNAL COURIER
      LPRINT E$;"&l0O";             ' PORTRAIT ORIENTATION
      LPRINT E$;"(8U";              ' ROMAN-8 SYMBOL SET
      LPRINT E$;"(s0p10h";          ' FIXED PITCH, 10 PITCH,
      LPRINT "12v0s";               ' 12 POINTS, UPRIGHT,
      LPRINT "0b3T";                ' NO BOLD, COURIER
      LPRINT CHR$(15);              ' SI TO ENSURE PRIMARY
                                    ' FONT WE JUST SELECTED

' SET LEFT MARGIN
      LPRINT E$;"&a10L";            ' SET LEFT MARGIN AT
                                    ' COLUMN 10

' SET RIGHT MARGIN
      LPRINT E$;"&a75M";            ' SET LEFT MARGIN AT
                                    ' COLUMN 75

' TURN PERFORATION SKIP ON
' -------------------------
      LPRINT E$;"&l1L";

END
```

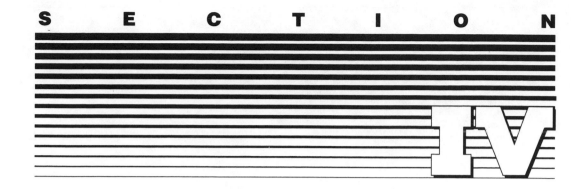

SECTION

IV

LASERJET + GRAPHICS

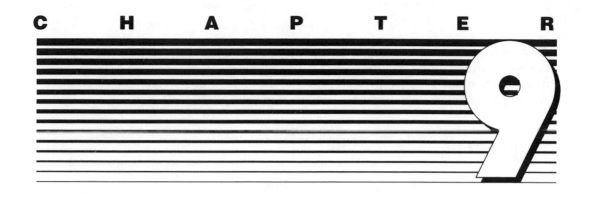

CHAPTER

9

RASTER GRAPHICS

A LaserJet+ compatible printer has two types of graphics capabilities. It can print **raster**, or **bit-mapped**, graphics, which specify each dot in a graphics pattern, or it can print **block graphics**, which print blocks of various patterns. This chapter covers raster graphics; Chapter 10 covers block graphics.

FOUR STEPS

There are four steps in printing raster graphics:

1. Set the graphics resolution.
2. Send the Start Graphics command.
3. Send the graphics data.
4. Send the End Graphics command.

Set Raster Graphics Resolution

Command	Explanation
ESC *t # R	# is 75, 100, 150, or 300

sets the dot resolution of the graphics, in dots per inch. Be sure to send this command before you send the Start Raster Graphics command because the printer will ignore this command once graphics have started.

Usually, you will send this command just before the Start Raster Graphics command (see next section), but this is not always necessary. You can send this command at any time, as long as it is before the Start Raster Graphics command.

If you don't specify a raster graphics resolution, the printer assumes you want 75 dots per inch.

Start Raster Graphics

Command	Explanation
ESC *r # A	# = 0 sets the graphics margin at the leftmost printable point on the page. Note that this point is not the same as the left margin, which is ignored in graphics mode. The graphics margin is *all the way* left.
	# = 1 sets the graphics margin at the current print position column. Each line of graphics will line up under the current position.

Send this command to begin sending graphics information to the printer.

Send Graphics Data

Send the following command at the beginning of each line of raster data.

Command	Explanation
ESC *b # W {data}	# is the number of bytes of graphics data that are to follow on this line. The curly brackets are not part of the command.

The data bytes are a bit map that describes the pattern of dots comprising the graphics pattern. They are read across the width of the page (raster graphics are always printed in portrait mode), starting on the current line at either the current column or the left-most printable position on the page, depending on how you set the Start Graphics command. If there is a dot in a location, the value of its bit is 1. If there is no dot, the bit's value is 0. Eight bits equal one byte.

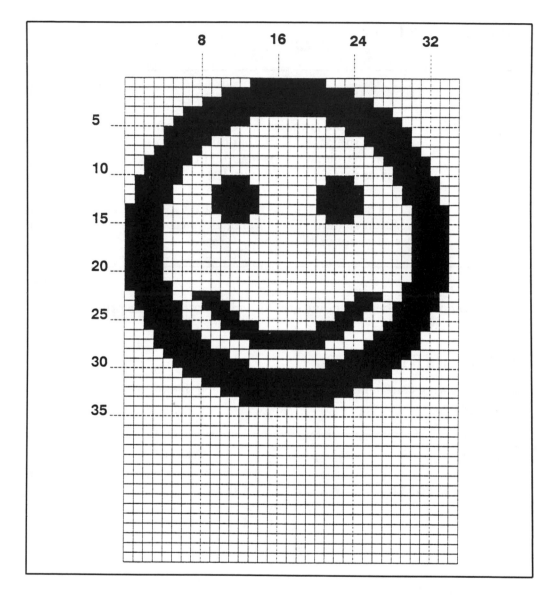

Figure 9.1   *Raster Graphics Example*

For example, in the happy face illustration in Figure 9.1, there are no dots in the first eight locations (from the upper left corner, reading across to the line marked 8), so the value of the first byte is

00000000

or 0$_D$.

In the next group of eight locations, the first five positions contain no dots, but there are dots in the next three positions, which together make a byte of

00000111

or 7$_D$ (ones in the 4s, 2s, and 1s columns).

The third byte is

1111000

or 248$_D$ (ones in the 128s, 64s, 32s, 16s, and 8s columns).

The fourth byte is 0$_D$.

The data bytes for the first five lines of the happy face are as follows:

1. 0_D, 7_D, 248_D, 0_D

2. 0_D, 63_D, 255_D, 0_D

3. 0_D, 255_D, 255_D, 192_D

4. 3_D, 255_D, 255_D, 240_D

5. 7_D, 248_D, 7_D, 248_D

There are 34 lines of data in the happy face. The first ten and last ten lines have only four bytes each; however, lines 11 through 24 each have five bytes because they each consist of more than 32 dots (32 bits = 4 bytes).

End Raster Graphics

Command	Explanation
ESC *r B	End raster graphics

Use this command to end raster graphics.

MEMORY CONSIDERATIONS IN RASTER GRAPHICS

Raster graphics consume huge amounts of memory. A megabyte of printer memory is required to handle a full page of raster graphics. Most laser printers do not contain that much memory to start with, though more memory can usually be added as an upgrade.

On most printers, the same memory used for raster graphics must also hold downloaded fonts. The more fonts loaded, the smaller the raster graphics you will be able to print.

As a result, you must carefully plan raster graphics to fit in available memory. In particular, designs with many vertical lines are extremely memory-intensive. Remember, the printer produces raster graphics by scanning from side to side. If you need two vertical lines 2" apart and 4" high, the printer must draw four square inches of raster graphics, even if the two lines are only a single dot wide.

Instead of using raster graphics for vertical lines, use the Block and Pattern Graphics outlined in Chapter 10.

RASTER GRAPHICS EXAMPLE PROGRAM

Following is an example of a raster graphics program. To adapt this program for your graphic image, replace the data lines with the picture you want to reproduce.

```
' ============= LOGO.BAS ===============
'
' THIS PROGRAM PRINTS THE MIS PRESS LOGO
' USING LASERJET+ RASTER GRAPHICS.
'
' YOU CAN EASILY ADAPT IT TO PRINT
' ANY GRAPHICS IMAGE AT ANY RESOLUTION
'
' =======================================

' PRELIMINARIES

' DECLARE SUBPROGRAMS AND FUNCTIONS
  DECLARE SUB Drawgraph (E$)
  DECLARE FUNCTION ConvertBinary% (DATA2$)

  E$  = CHR$(27)    ' ESCAPE CHARACTER
  FF$ = CHR$(12)    ' FORM FEED CHARACTER
  LF$ = CHR$(10)    ' LINE FEED CHARACTER
```

continued...

...from previous page

```
' SETUP PRINTER
  OPEN "LPT1:" FOR OUTPUT AS #1        ' OPEN PRINTER AS FILE
  WIDTH "LPT1:", 255
  PRINT #1, E$; "E"                    ' RESET
  PRINT #1, E$; "&l0C"                 ' SET LINE SPACING TO 0

' MOVE TO CENTER OF PAGE
  PRINT #1, E$; "*p300x300Y";

' SET RASTER GRAPHICS RESOLUTION
  PRINT #1, E$; "*t100R";

' PRINT THE GRAPHIC
  CALL Drawgraph(E$)                   ' THIS PRINTS THE
                                       ' GRAPHIC

PRINT #1, E$; "E                       ' RESET PRINTER AND
                                       ' EJECT PAGE
CLOSE #1                               ' CLOSE FILE (PRINTER)
' ----------------------------------------------------
'
' THESE DATA LINES CONTAIN THE ACTUAL DATA FOR
' THE PICTURE.  # MEANS A DOT IN THAT LOCATION.
' ANYTHING ELSE MEANS NO DOT
'
' EACH LINE OF DATA MUST CONTAIN A NUMBER OF CHARACTERS THAT
' IS AN EXACT MULTIPLE OF EIGHT.  IN ORDER TO FORMAT THIS
' EXAMPLE SO TI WOULD FIT ON THE PAGE, IT DOES NOT HAVE A
' MULTIPLE OF EIGHT CHARACTERS ON EACH LINE.  TO RUN
' CORRECTLY, IT MUST.  IF YOU ARE GOING TO KEY THIS PROGRAM
' IN AND RUN IT, ADD 10 CHARACTER TO THE BEGINNING OF EACH
' LINE.
'
' THE LAST LINE OF THE DATA MUST READ "END OF DATA".
'
' ----------------------------------------------------
```

continued...

...from previous page

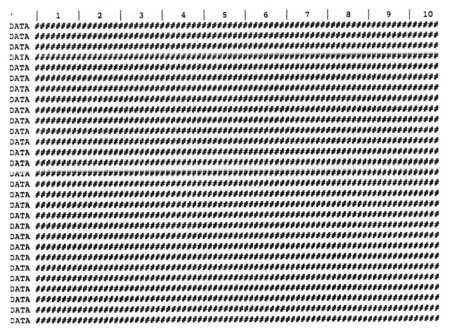

continued...

...from previous page

```
DATA ####################################################################
DATA ####################################################################
DATA ####################################################################
DATA ########            ##########         ##       #####        ##      ###########
DATA ########            ##########         ##       ####         #       ###########
DATA ##########          #######          ######     #####      ###      ####     ####
DATA ##########           #######         #######     ####      #####     ###      ###
DATA ##########      #    #######    #     #######     ####     #######     ###      ###
DATA ##########      #    #######    #     #######     ####     ########     ###      ###
DATA ##########     ##    #####    ##      #######     ####     #########     ####    ####
DATA ##########     ##    #####    ##      #######     ####     ###########
DATA ##########     ##    #####    ##      #######     ####     ###############
DATA ##########     ###    ####    ###     #######     ####     ################
DATA ##########     ###    ####    ###     #######     #####     #################
DATA ##########     ###    ####    ###     #######     #####      ################
DATA ##########     ####     ####          #######     #######      ##############
DATA ##########     ####     ##    ###     #######     ########       ###########
DATA ##########     ####     ##    ###     #######     ##############     ##########
DATA ##########     ####          ####     #######     ################     ########
DATA ##########     ####          ####     #######     ################       #######
DATA ##########     #####          ####     #######     ################       #######
DATA ##########     #####          #####     #######     ###############        ######
DATA ##########     ######          #####     #######     ####                #####
DATA ##########     #######          ######     #######     ####                #####     ##
DATA ##########     #######          ######     #######     ####                ####      ##
DATA ########          ####     #######     ####          #    #                #####     ##
DATA ########          #########          ##            ##    ###      ########      ###
DATA ####################################################################
DATA ####################################################################
DATA ····················································································
DATA ####################################################################
DATA ###          ########          ########          ########          ##########          ####
DATA ###          #######          ########          #######          ########          ###
DATA ###    ####    #######    ####    #######    #############    ###    ########    ###    ####
DATA ###    ####    #######    ####    #######    #############    ###########    #######
DATA ###          ########          #######          #############    ###########    #####
DATA ###          ########          #######          #############    ##########    ####
DATA ###    #############    ##    #########    ################    ###########    ##
DATA ###    #############    ###    ########    ##############    ####    ########    ####    ##
DATA ###    #############    ###    ########    ##############    ####    #######    ####    ###
DATA ###    #############    ####    #######    ########          #######          ###
DATA ####################################################################
DATA ····················································································
DATA ####################################################################
DATA ####################################################################
```

continued...

...from previous page

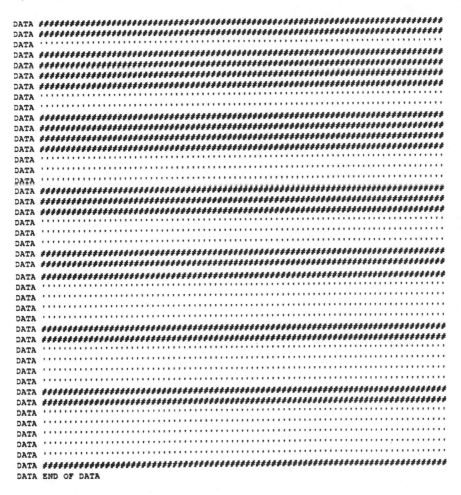

```
DATA ###########################################################################
DATA ###########################################################################
DATA · · · · · · · · · · · · · · · · · · · · · · · · · · · · · · · · · · · · · · ·
DATA ###########################################################################
DATA ###########################################################################
DATA ###########################################################################
DATA ###########################################################################
DATA · · · · · · · · · · · · · · · · · · · · · · · · · · · · · · · · · · · · · · ·
DATA · · · · · · · · · · · · · · · · · · · · · · · · · · · · · · · · · · · · · · ·
DATA ###########################################################################
DATA ###########################################################################
DATA ###########################################################################
DATA · · · · · · · · · · · · · · · · · · · · · · · · · · · · · · · · · · · · · · ·
DATA · · · · · · · · · · · · · · · · · · · · · · · · · · · · · · · · · · · · · · ·
DATA · · · · · · · · · · · · · · · · · · · · · · · · · · · · · · · · · · · · · · ·
DATA ###########################################################################
DATA ###########################################################################
DATA ###########################################################################
DATA · · · · · · · · · · · · · · · · · · · · · · · · · · · · · · · · · · · · · · ·
DATA · · · · · · · · · · · · · · · · · · · · · · · · · · · · · · · · · · · · · · ·
DATA · · · · · · · · · · · · · · · · · · · · · · · · · · · · · · · · · · · · · · ·
DATA ###########################################################################
DATA ###########################################################################
DATA ###########################################################################
DATA · · · · · · · · · · · · · · · · · · · · · · · · · · · · · · · · · · · · · · ·
DATA · · · · · · · · · · · · · · · · · · · · · · · · · · · · · · · · · · · · · · ·
DATA · · · · · · · · · · · · · · · · · · · · · · · · · · · · · · · · · · · · · · ·
DATA · · · · · · · · · · · · · · · · · · · · · · · · · · · · · · · · · · · · · · ·
DATA ###########################################################################
DATA ###########################################################################
DATA · · · · · · · · · · · · · · · · · · · · · · · · · · · · · · · · · · · · · · ·
DATA · · · · · · · · · · · · · · · · · · · · · · · · · · · · · · · · · · · · · · ·
DATA · · · · · · · · · · · · · · · · · · · · · · · · · · · · · · · · · · · · · · ·
DATA · · · · · · · · · · · · · · · · · · · · · · · · · · · · · · · · · · · · · · ·
DATA ###########################################################################
DATA ###########################################################################
DATA · · · · · · · · · · · · · · · · · · · · · · · · · · · · · · · · · · · · · · ·
DATA · · · · · · · · · · · · · · · · · · · · · · · · · · · · · · · · · · · · · · ·
DATA · · · · · · · · · · · · · · · · · · · · · · · · · · · · · · · · · · · · · · ·
DATA · · · · · · · · · · · · · · · · · · · · · · · · · · · · · · · · · · · · · · ·
DATA · · · · · · · · · · · · · · · · · · · · · · · · · · · · · · · · · · · · · · ·
DATA ###########################################################################
DATA END OF DATA
```

continued...

...from previous page

```
END

'
'
'  ------------ConvertBinary%---------------
'
' THIS FUNCTION CONVERTS A STRING CONTAINING
' # CHARACTERS INTO A DECIMAL NUMBER.  A # IN
' ANY POSITION MEANS THE VALUE OF THAT POSITION
' IS A 1.  ANYTHING ELSE IS A 0.
'
' -----------------------------------------
'
FUNCTION ConvertBinary% (DATA2$)

   BinVALUE% = 0
   BINARYCOUNTER% = 1

   FOR Z% = 8 TO 1 STEP -1
      IF MID$(DATA2$, Z%, 1) = "#" THEN
      ' ADD VALUE OF PLACE
         BinVALUE% = BinVALUE% + BINARYCOUNTER%
      END IF
   BINARYCOUNTER% = BINARYCOUNTER% * 2    ' INCREMENT BINARY
                                          ' PLACE VALUE
   NEXT Z%
   ConvertBinary% = BinVALUE%

END FUNCTION

'
' -------------- DRAWGRAPH ------------------
'
' THIS SUBPROGRAM ACTUALLY DRAWS THE GRAPHICS
'
' -----------------------------------------
'
SUB Drawgraph (E$) STATIC
```

continued...

continued...

```
PRINT #1, E$; "*r1A";              ' START GRAPHICS AT
                                   ' CURRENT COLUMN
RESTORE                            ' START READING FROM
                                   ' BEGINNING OF DATA

DO WHILE DATA$ <> "END OF DATA"    ' STOPS AT END OF
                                   ' PICTURE

  ' READ ONE LINE OF DOT PATTERNS FROM DATA STATEMENTS
    READ DATA$

  ' DISCARD THE LINE NUMBER
    DATA1$ = RIGHT$(DATA$, LEN(DATA$) - 4)


  ' HOW MANY BYTES IN THE LINE?
    NUMBYTES% = LEN(DATA1$) / 8     ' HOW MANY BYTES?
    NUMBYTES$ = STR$(NUMBYTES%)     ' CONVERT TO
                                    ' STRING
  ' STRIP OFF LEADING BLANK SPACE
    NUMBYTES$ = RIGHT$(NUMBYTES$, LEN(NUMBYTES$) - 1)

  ' START LINE OF GRAPHICS
    PRINT #1, E$; "*b"; NUMBYTES$; "W";

  ' PRINT GRAPHICS DATA
    FOR Y% = 1 TO 88 STEP 8
       DATA2$ = MID$(DATA1$, Y%, 8)     ' READ 8
                                        ' CHARACTERS
    DATATOPRINT% = ConvertBinary%(DATA2$)
                                        ' CONVERT TO
                                        ' DECIMAL NUMBER
    PRINT #1, CHR$(DATATOPRINT%);       ' PRINT IT
  NEXT Y%

LOOP

PRINT #1, E$; "*rB                      ' END GRAPHICS
END SUB
```

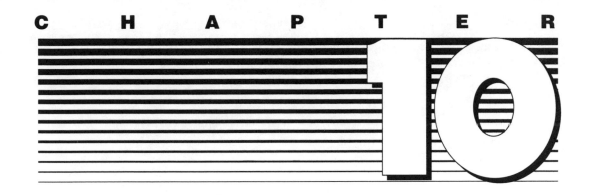

C H A P T E R

10

BLOCK AND PATTERN GRAPHICS

Using block and pattern graphics, you can easily print blocks filled with a particular pattern. There are three steps in the process:

1. Specify the block dimensions.

2. Select the pattern to fill the block.

3. Print the block.

SPECIFY BLOCK DIMENSIONS

The following commands set the block size measured in dots (300 dots per inch).

Command	Explanation
ESC *c # A	Horizontal size of block in dots
ESC *c # B	Vertical size of block in dots

The following commands set the block size, measured in decipoints (720 decipoints per inch).

Command	Explanation
ESC *c # H	Horizontal size of block in decipoints
ESC *c # V	Vertical size of block in decipoints

Both sets of commands specify a block measured to the right and down from the current print position.

If you specify a block larger than the page, the printer will accept the command but clip off the block at the edges of the page; in other words, the printer will not carry the block onto another page.

The printer converts decipoint values to dots, with fractions rounded up to the next integer. The conversion factor is 2.4 decipoints per dot; for example, 1459 decipoints calculates to 607.92 dots, and the printer rounds this value up to 608 dots.

Blocks and Lines

If you want to print line graphics, direct print-positioning commands and narrow, long blocks use the printer's memory much more efficiently than raster graphics. (If your printer also includes the IBM character set with characters such as ┤, │, and ┬, you can often construct the line graphics you need from these line-drawing characters. Also, Hewlett-Packard provides a special font named Tax Draw, which contains nothing but line-drawing characters.

SELECT BLOCK PATTERN

Command	Explanation
ESC *c # G	Select block pattern

This command sets the pattern to fill the block. Values of # from 1 to 6 can specify either ruling patterns of lines or gray scale patterns, depending on the print-block command (see Figure 10.1). Values from 7 to 100 specify dot patterns only.

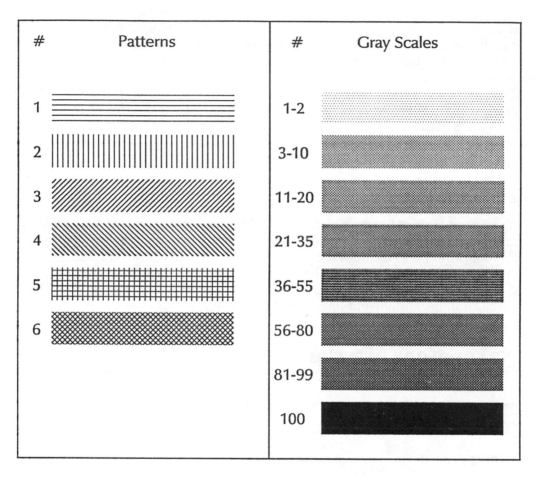

Figure 10.1   *Patterns and Gray Scales Accessible from the Select Block Pattern Command*

PRINT BLOCK

Command	Explanation
ESC *c # P	# = 0 overrides the Select Block Pattern command and prints a black box. # = 1 prints a gray scale block. # = 2 prints a ruling pattern block. If the value of # in the Select Block Pattern command is greater than 6, the printer ignores this command.

This command prints the block and pattern graphic specified by the previous two commands.

EXAMPLE BLOCK AND PATTERN GRAPHICS PROGRAM

The following program prints a sheet covered by a grid (see Figure 10.2), which you can use to design characters and graphics.

You could use this grid with an enlarged photocopy of a design you want to digitize.

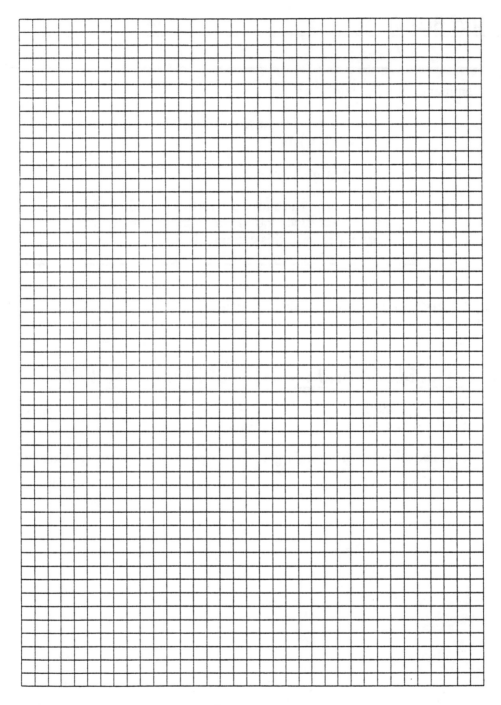

Figure 10.2   Grid created by Grid.bas program

```
' =============== GRID.BAS =================
'
' THIS PROGRAM PRODUCES A GRID ON WHICH YOU
' CAN DESIGN GRAPHICS AND FONT CHARACTERS
'
' =========================================

' --- PRELIMINARIES ---

  E$ = CHR$(27)                        ' ESCAPE CHARACTER
  FF$ = CHR$(12)                       ' FORM FEED CHARACTER
  LF$ = CHR$(10)                       ' LINE FEED CHARACTER

' --- SETUP PRINTER ---
  OPEN "LPT1:" FOR OUTPUT AS #1        ' OPEN PRINTER AS FILE
  WIDTH "LPT1:", 255                   ' OVERRIDE AUTO CR/LF
  PRINT #1, E$; "E";                   ' RESET

' --- MAKE SURE AT START POINT ---
  PRINT #1, E$; "*p150x150Y";

' --- VERTICAL LINES ---

  FOR V = 0 TO 72
    IF V MOD 8 = 0 THEN
      PRINT #1, E$; "*c5a2850b0P"; ' WIDER LINE EVERY 8TH
    ELSE
      PRINT #1, E$; "*c1a2850b0P"; ' NORMAL LINE OTHERS
    END IF
    PRINT #1, E$; "*p+30X";            ' MOVE TO NEXT COLUMN
  NEXT V

' --- RETURN TO START POINT ---
  PRINT #1, E$; "*p150x150Y";
```

continued...

...from previous page

```
' --- HORIZONTAL LINES ---

  FOR H = 0 TO 95
    IF H MOD 5 = 0 THEN
      PRINT #1, E$; "*c2160a5b0P"; ' WIDER LINE EVERY 5TH
    ELSE
      PRINT #1, E$; "*c2160a1b0P"; ' NORMAL LINE OTHERS
    END IF
    PRINT #1, E$; "*p+30Y";         ' MOVE TO NEXT ROW
  NEXT H


  PRINT #1, FF$
  CLOSE #1

  END
```

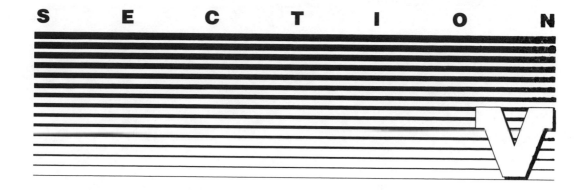

S E C T I O N

V

MACROS AND MISCELLANEOUS COMMANDS

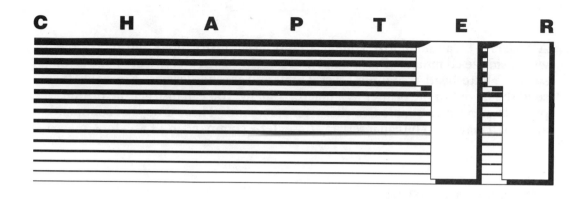

LASERJET + MACROS

A LaserJet+ can memorize complicated printing instructions and replay them with a simple command. For example, you could design an intricate page layout, such as a letterhead, containing several fonts and graphic designs. You could then send the layout to the printer as a macro. Finally, you can instruct the printer to print it again with a simple five-character command. These groups of commands are called **macros**. You can insert any LaserJet+ command in a LaserJet+ macro.

SPECIFY MACRO ID

The following command sets the macro ID number for the next macro operation of the Macro Control command:

Command	Explanation
ESC &f # Y	Set macro ID to #

For example, if you wanted to delete a macro numbered 100, you would send the printer the command ESC &f 100 Y followed by the Delete Macro command, ESC &f 8 X.

MACRO CONTROL

Use the following command to control macros:

```
Command        Explanation

ESC &f # X     #   Action
               0   Start Macro Definition
               1   End Macro Definition
               2   Execute Macro
               3   Call Macro
               4   Auto Macro Overlay ON
               5   Auto Macro Overlay OFF
               6   Delete All Macros
               7   Delete Temporary Macros
               8   Delete Most Recent Macro
               9   Make Most Recent Macro Temporary
              10   Make Most Recent Macro Permanent
```

Following are detailed explanations of each of the Macro Control commands:

 # = 0   **Start Macro Definition.** This command creates a new temporary macro with the macro number most recently specified by the Specify Macro ID command (ESC &f # Y).

The printer will memorize the sequence of commands until it receives the End Macro Definition command. LaserJet+ macros can contain any valid LaserJet+ commands (except, of course, the End Macro Definition command.)

Because the new macro created with this command is temporary, it can be erased by a Printer Reset command (ESC E). If you want to make the macro permanent, use the command ESC &f 10 X after you have finished defining the macro.

 # = 1   **End Macro Definition.** Send this command after you have finished sending to the printer the sequence of commands you want in the macro.

 # = 2   **Execute Macro.** When the printer receives this command, it executes the most recently specified macro, modifying the printer environment according to the macro's instructions.

The parameters of the printer environment are as follows:

<u>Parameters</u>

Page Length   Character Code
Orientation   Macro ID Number
Paper Cassette   Horizontal Motion Index (HMI)
Number of Copies   Vertical Motion Index (VMI)
Top and Bottom Margins   Underline Mode
Left and Right Margins   Raster Graphics
Perforation Skip Status   Mode
Line Termination Function   Resolution
End-of-Line Wrap Status   Margin
Font Attributes   Block Graphics Pattern
Font ID   Overlay
Font Primary Address   Print Position (Cursor) Stack

= 3   **Call Macro.** Like the Execute Macro command, this command executes the most recently specified macro. In this case, however, the printer first saves its environment and then restores it after the macro is finished.

= 4   **Auto Macro Overlay ON.** When you turn the Auto Macro Overlay ON, the printer prints the most recently specified macro automatically on every page until the printer receives the Auto Macro Overlay OFF command (ESC &f 5 X). Changing page length or orientation also cancels an Auto Macro Overlay. The printer restores the environment after Auto Macro Overlay execution.

Use this command if you want the same design reproduced on each page.

= 5   **Auto Macro Overlay OFF.** Turns the Auto Macro Overlay feature OFF, starting with the current page. Changing page length or orientation also cancels an Auto Macro Overlay.

= 6   **Delete All Macros.** Deletes all macros, including permanent macros and Auto Macro Overlays.

= 7   **Delete Temporary Macros.** Deletes all temporary macros, including temporary auto macros.

= 8   **Delete Most Recently Specified Macro.**

= 9   **Make Most Recently Specified Macro Temporary.**

= 10   **Make Most Recently Specified Macro Permanent.**

SAMPLE MACRO PROGRAM

The following macro stores the MIS:PRESS logo designed in Chapter 9 as a macro:

```
'
' ============= MACRO.BAS ===============
'
' THIS PROGRAM STORES THE MIS PRESS LOGO
' AS A LASERJET+ MACRO.
'
' ==========================================



' ---   PRELIMINARIES   ---

' DECLARE SUBPROGRAMS AND FUNCTIONS
  DECLARE SUB Drawgraph (E$)
  DECLARE FUNCTION ConvertBinary% (DATA2$)

  E$  = CHR$(27)                 ' ESCAPE CHARACTER
  FF$ = CHR$(12)                 ' FORM FEED CHARACTER
  LF$ = CHR$(10)                 ' LINE FEED CHARACTER
```

continued...

...from previous page

```
' SETUP PRINTER
  OPEN "LPT1:" FOR OUTPUT AS #1      ' OPEN PRINTER AS FILE
  WIDTH "LPT1:", 255
  PRINT #1, E$; "E";                 ' RESET
  PRINT #1, E$; "&l0C";              ' SET LINE SPACING TO 0

  PRINT #1, E$; "&f10y0X";           ' ASSIGN MACRO NUMBER
                                     ' (10) AND START
                                     '  DEFINITION

' ------BEGINNING OF MACRO DEFINITION-------

' SET RASTER GRAPHICS RESOLUTION
  PRINT #1, E$; "*t100R";

' PRINT THE GRAPHIC
  CALL Drawgraph(E$)                 ' THIS PRINTS THE
                                     ' GRAPHIC

' ------------ END OF MACRO DEFINITION ----------

  PRINT #1, E$; "&f1X"               ' END MACRO DEFINITION

' ---- SHOW OFF THE MACRO IN DIFFERENT POSITIONS ----

' MOVE TO RIGHT TOP SIDE OF PAGE
  PRINT #1, E$; "*p1500x600Y";

  PRINT #1, E$; "&f2X";              ' EXECUTE MACRO

' MOVE TO LOWER LEFT SIDE OF PAGE
  PRINT #1, E$; "*p450x2400Y";

  PRINT #1, E$; "&f2X";              ' EXECUTE MACRO AGAIN

  PRINT #1, E$; "E"                  ' RESET PRINTER AND
                                     ' EJECT PAGE
  CLOSE #1                           ' CLOSE FILE (PRINTER)
```

continued...

...from previous page

```
' ------------------------------------------------------
'
' THESE DATA LINES CONTAIN THE ACTUAL DATA FOR
' THE PICTURE.  # MEANS A DOT IN THAT LOCATION.
' ANYTHING ELSE MEANS NO DOT
'
' EACH LINE OF DATA MUST CONTAIN A NUMBER OF CHARACTERS THAT
' IS AN EXACT MULTIPLE OF EIGHT.  IN ORDER TO FORMAT THIS
' EXAMPLE SO TI WOULD FIT ON THE PAGE, IT DOES NOT HAVE A
' MULTIPLE OF EIGHT CHARACTERS ON EACH LINE.  TO RUN
' CORRECTLY, IT MUST.  IF YOU ARE GOING TO KEY THIS PROGRAM
' IN AND RUN IT, ADD 10 CHARACTER TO THE BEGINNING OF EACH
' LINE.
'
' THE LAST LINE OF THE DATA MUST READ "END OF DATA".
'
' ------------------------------------------------------
```

```
'     |  1  |  2  |  3  |  4  |  5  |  6  |  7  |  8  |  9  | 10
DATA ####################################################################
DATA ####################################################################
DATA ####################################################################
DATA ####################################################################
DATA ####################################################################
DATA ####################################################################
DATA ####################################################################
DATA ####################################################################
DATA ####################################################################
DATA ####################################################################
DATA ####################################################################
DATA ####################################################################
DATA ####################################################################
DATA ####################################################################
DATA ####################################################################
DATA ####################################################################
DATA ####################################################################
DATA ####################################################################
DATA ####################################################################
DATA ####################################################################
DATA ####################################################################
DATA ####################################################################
DATA ####################################################################
DATA ####################################################################
DATA ####################################################################
DATA ####################################################################
DATA ####################################################################
DATA ####################################################################
DATA ####################################################################
```

continued...

...from previous page

```
DATA ##################################################################
DATA ##################################################################
DATA #######          ##########         ##        #####        #     ##########
DATA #######          #########          ##        ###    '        ##########
DATA #########         ########          #######    ####       ##      ####    ####
DATA #########         #######           #######    ####       ##      ##      ###
DATA #########    #    #######    #       #######    ###    ######    ##      ###
DATA #########    #    #######    #       #######    ###    ######    ##      ###
DATA #########    ##    #####     ##      #######    ###    ########    ###    ####
DATA #########    ##    #####     ##      #######    ###    ##########    ####    #######
DATA #########    ##    #####     ##      #######    ###    ##########    ###
DATA #########    ###    ####     ###     #######    ####    ##########    #############
DATA #########    ###    ####     ###     #######    #####    #############
DATA #########    ###    ##    ####     #######    #######    #############
DATA #########    ###    ##    ####     #######    #######    #############
DATA #########    ####    ####     ####     #######    ##########    #############
DATA #########    ####    ####     ####     #######    ##############    #######
DATA #########    ####    ####     #######    #######    ####    ########    #######
DATA #########    #####    #####     #######    ####    ########    #######
DATA #########    #####    #####     #######    ####    ########    ###    #
DATA #########    #####    #####     #######    ####    #####    ###    ##
DATA #########    ######    #####     #######    ####    #####    ###    ##
DATA #########          ####    #######    #####          #    #    #####    ##
DATA #######          #########          ##          #    ##    ########    #
DATA ##################################################################
DATA ##################################################################
DATA ..................................................................
DATA ##################################################################
DATA ###      ########      ########          ########    ##########    #####
DATA ###      ########      ########          ########    #########    ####
DATA ###    ####    ########    ####    ########    ##########    ###    ########    ###    ###
DATA ###    ####    ########    ####    ########    ##########    ###    ########    ###    #######
DATA ###    ####    ########    ####    ########    ##########    ###    #########    #######
DATA ###          ########          ########    ###########    ##########    ####
DATA ###          ########          ########    #############    ##########    ###
DATA ###    #############    ##    ########    ###############    #############    ##
DATA ###    #############    ###    ########    ###############    ####    #######    ###    ##
DATA ###    #############    ####    ########          #######          #######    ##
DATA ###    #############    ####    ########          #######          ########    ###
DATA ###    #############    ####    ########          #######          ########    ##
DATA ##################################################################
DATA ..................................................................
DATA ##################################################################
DATA ##################################################################
DATA ##################################################################
DATA ##################################################################
DATA ..................................................................
DATA ##################################################################
DATA ##################################################################
DATA ##################################################################
DATA ##################################################################
```

continued...

...from previous page

```
DATA ''''''''''''''''''''''''''''''''''''''''''''''''''''''''''''''''''''''''''''
DATA ''''''''''''''''''''''''''''''''''''''''''''''''''''''''''''''''''''''''''''
DATA ############################################################################
DATA ############################################################################
DATA ############################################################################
DATA ############################################################################
DATA ''''''''''''''''''''''''''''''''''''''''''''''''''''''''''''''''''''''''''''
DATA ''''''''''''''''''''''''''''''''''''''''''''''''''''''''''''''''''''''''''''
DATA ''''''''''''''''''''''''''''''''''''''''''''''''''''''''''''''''''''''''''''
DATA ############################################################################
DATA ############################################################################
DATA ############################################################################
DATA ''''''''''''''''''''''''''''''''''''''''''''''''''''''''''''''''''''''''''''
DATA ''''''''''''''''''''''''''''''''''''''''''''''''''''''''''''''''''''''''''''
DATA ''''''''''''''''''''''''''''''''''''''''''''''''''''''''''''''''''''''''''''
DATA ############################################################################
DATA ############################################################################
DATA ############################################################################
DATA ''''''''''''''''''''''''''''''''''''''''''''''''''''''''''''''''''''''''''''
DATA ''''''''''''''''''''''''''''''''''''''''''''''''''''''''''''''''''''''''''''
DATA ''''''''''''''''''''''''''''''''''''''''''''''''''''''''''''''''''''''''''''
DATA ''''''''''''''''''''''''''''''''''''''''''''''''''''''''''''''''''''''''''''
DATA ############################################################################
DATA ############################################################################
DATA ''''''''''''''''''''''''''''''''''''''''''''''''''''''''''''''''''''''''''''
DATA ''''''''''''''''''''''''''''''''''''''''''''''''''''''''''''''''''''''''''''
DATA ''''''''''''''''''''''''''''''''''''''''''''''''''''''''''''''''''''''''''''
DATA ''''''''''''''''''''''''''''''''''''''''''''''''''''''''''''''''''''''''''''
DATA ############################################################################
DATA ############################################################################
DATA ''''''''''''''''''''''''''''''''''''''''''''''''''''''''''''''''''''''''''''
DATA ''''''''''''''''''''''''''''''''''''''''''''''''''''''''''''''''''''''''''''
DATA ''''''''''''''''''''''''''''''''''''''''''''''''''''''''''''''''''''''''''''
DATA ''''''''''''''''''''''''''''''''''''''''''''''''''''''''''''''''''''''''''''
DATA ############################################################################
DATA END OF DATA

END

'
' ------------ConvertBinary%---------------
'
' THIS FUNCTION CONVERTS A STRING CONTAINING
' # CHARACTERS INTO A DECIMAL NUMBER.  A # IN
' ANY POSITION MEANS THE VALUE OF THAT POSITION
' IS A 1.  ANYTHING ELSE IS A 0.
'
' -------------------------------------------
```

continued...

...from previous page

```
FUNCTION ConvertBinary% (DATA2$)

   BinVALUE% = 0
   BINARYCOUNTER% = 1

   FOR Z% = 8 TO 1 STEP -1
      IF MID$(DATA2$, Z%, 1) = "#" THEN
      ' ADD VALUE OF PLACE
         BinVALUE% = BinVALUE% + BINARYCOUNTER%
      END IF
   BINARYCOUNTER% = BINARYCOUNTER% * 2    ' INCREMENT BINARY
                                          ' PLACE VALUE
   NEXT Z%
   ConvertBinary% = BinVALUE%

END FUNCTION

'
' -------------- DRAWGRAPH -------------------
'
' THIS SUBPROGRAM ACTUALLY DRAWS THE GRAPHICS
'
' --------------------------------------------
'
SUB Drawgraph (E$) STATIC

PRINT #1, E$; "*r1A";                 ' START GRAPHICS AT
                                      ' CURRENT COLUMN
RESTORE                               ' START READING FROM
                                      ' BEGINNING OF DATA

DO WHILE DATA$ <> "END OF DATA"       ' STOPS AT END OF
                                      ' PICTURE

   ' READ ONE LINE OF DOT PATTERNS FROM DATA STATEMENTS
     READ DATA$

   ' DISCARD THE LINE NUMBER
     DATA1$ = RIGHT$(DATA$, LEN(DATA$) - 4)
```

continued...

...from previous page

```
' HOW MANY BYTES IN THE LINE?
  NUMBYTES% = LEN(DATA1$) / 8      ' HOW MANY BYTES?
  NUMBYTES$ = STR$(NUMBYTES%)       ' CONVERT TO STRING
  NUMBYTES$ = RIGHT$(NUMBYTES$, LEN(NUMBYTES$) - 1)
                                    ' STRIP OFF
                                    ' LEADING
                                    ' BLANK SPACE

' START LINE OF GRAPHICS
  PRINT #1, E$; "*b"; NUMBYTES$; "W";

' PRINT GRAPHICS DATA
  FOR Y% = 1 TO 88 STEP 8
     DATA2$ = MID$(DATA1$, Y%, 8)            ' READ 8
     DATATOPRINT% = ConvertBinary%(DATA2$)
                                             ' CONVERT TO
                                             ' DECIMAL NUMBER
     PRINT #1, CHR$(DATATOPRINT%);           ' PRINT IT
   NEXT Y%

LOOP

PRINT #1, E$; "*rB                           ' END GRAPHICS
END SUB
```

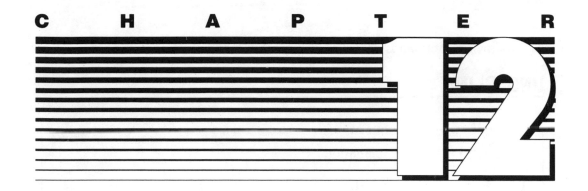

MISCELLANEOUS COMMANDS

The following commands do not fit in any other category.

UNDERLINE

Command	Explanation
ESC &d D	Underline ON
ESC &d @	Underline OFF

When underline mode is ON, all characters, including spaces, are underlined.

RESET PRINTER

Command	Explanation
ESC E	Printer reset

This command prints any page in the printer and resets all printer parameters back to their defaults.

Printer Defaults

Following are the default values for a Hewlett-Packard LaserJet+. They may vary on some compatible printers; see your printer manual. Also, many printers allow you to change the defaults and save those new default values in a special section of permanent memory in the printer.

When writing programs that you expect to run on compatible printers, never assume any of these values; always explicitly instruct the printer as to what value you want for each of these parameters.

Margins:
Top - 3 lines
Bottom - 3 lines
Right - right edge of paper
Left - left edge of paper
Underlining:
OFF
Primary/Secondary Fonts:
(same settings)
Portrait Orientation
Roman-8 Symbol Set
10 Pitch
12 Points
Upright Style
Medium Weight
Courier Typeface
(Resident Courier)
Line Spacing:
6 lines per inch
Raster Graphics Resolution:
75 dots per inch

Horizontal Motion Index:
1/10" (12/120")
Display Functions:
OFF
Perforation Skip Mode:
Enabled
Line Termination:
CR, LF, and FF all print as sent
End of Line Wrap:
Disabled
Orientation:
Portrait
Number of Copies:
One
Paper Input Control:
Feed from Cassette (upper cassette if more than one installed)

Figure 12.1   Printer Defaults for Hewlett-Packard Laser Jet +

Fixed Starting Position

It is possible to fix the starting print position by sending the printer a reset command and then sending it a command that sets (a) page length, (b) orientation, (c) top margin, (d) left margin, (e) vertical motion index, or (f) line spacing. As long as the printer receives one of these commands before a command moving the print position or any printable characters, the starting position will be fixed.

The results of a fixed starting position are as follows:

- The current print position is not affected by changes to the top or left margins, the VMI, or line spacing.

- Once the starting position is fixed, the printer will eject the page if it receives a command to change the page length or orientation.

SELF-TEST

Command	Explanation
ESC z	Self-Test

When the printer receives this command, it immediately prints any page in progress, ejects it, and then tests the printer interface. If the printer finds no problems, it is ready to receive more data. If it finds an error, it goes off line. Details on how to correct interface problems for a particular printer can usually be found in the printer's documentation.

NUMBER OF COPIES

Command	Explanation
ESC &l # X	# = number of copies to print of each page

PAPER INPUT CONTROL

The following command takes effect on the current page and stays in effect until you send the printer a new Number of Copies command or change the number of copies through the front panel switches.

Command	Explanation	
<u>ESC</u> &l # H	<u>#</u>	<u>Action</u>
	0	Ejects the current page; this is the same as a form feed.
	1	Feeds paper from the upper paper cassette tray.
	2	Feeds paper from the manual input slot.
	3	Feeds an envelope from the manual input slot.
	4	Feeds paper from the lower paper cassette tray on printers with two trays.

With most printers, there is no difference between feeding paper and feeding an envelope from the manual feed tray.

Shifting Paper Sizes

On some compatible printers, the printer assumes a different paper size when you feed paper from the manual paper feed slot. As one printer company engineer explained, "We assumed that if you were using the manual paper feed, you weren't feeding normal-sized paper." On that particular printer (the Mannesmann-Tally MT910), the default paper size (if you are using the manual paper feed slot) is 8.5" × 14". Other printers may rely on similar assumptions.

This fact presents particular problems when you want to print in landscape orientation, such as when addressing an envelope. Remember, in landscape mode, the origin is on the trailing edge of the paper (the last edge of the paper to pass through the printer). (See Figure 12.2.)

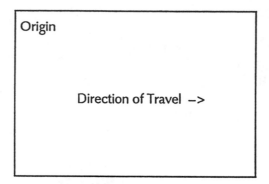

Figure 12.2   *Envelope Printing in Landscape Mode*

Imagine that you are printing on an envelope and you can see that the trailing edge of a 14" sheet of paper is well beyond the left margin of the envelope (see Figure 12.3).

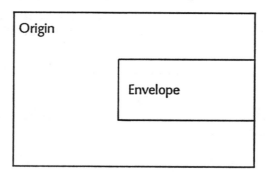

Figure 12.3   *Envelope Printing on 14" Paper*

Make no assumptions about the default paper sizes your printer uses. If you want to use the manual sheet feeder, use the paper size commands to inform the printer of the paper's exact size.

DISPLAY FUNCTIONS

Command	Explanation
ESC Y	Display Functions ON
ESC Z	Display Functions OFF

In Display Functions mode, the printer does not execute any commands except CR, which causes it to perform a carriage return and line feed, and ESC Z, which causes it to print a space and a Z and then leave the Display Functions mode. All other commands are printed as blanks.

TRANSPARENT PRINT DATA

Command	Explanation
ESC &p # X	# specifies the number of "transparent" bytes of data that are to follow.

In Transparent Print Data mode, the printer does not execute any control codes or escape sequences for # bytes.

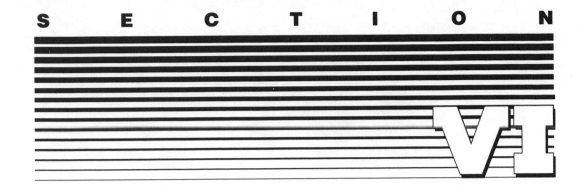

SECTION VI

LASERJET + COMPATIBLE PRINTERS

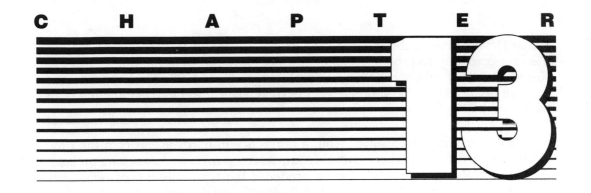

ALTERNATIVES
TO HEWLETT-PACKARD

When Hewlett-Packard introduced the original LaserJet in 1984, they were not the first company to produce a computer laser printer. That honor belongs to Xerox, which brought out the model 9700 laser printer in 1977. The big difference was the price. The 9700 retailed for $350,000. The LaserJet cost about 1% of that price.

The difference in price resulted from a difference in hardware. From the time Xerox's 9700 hit the market, several Japanese companies were working on laser printing technology. In 1983, Canon produced the first truly inexpensive laser printer engine — the LBP-CX. Hewlett-Packard picked them up from Japan for less than $1,000 each. Adding in their own circuitry board to make the engine perform, they produced the first inexpensive laser printer.

PRINTER CONTROL LANGUAGE

As part of this project, Hewlett-Packard developed a new printer control language referred to as Printer Control Language (PCL). Hewlett-Packard now uses this language in all its printers — not just in the LaserJet family.

Once Hewlett-Packard defined the PCL, other manufacturers began creating printers that responded to the same set of commands. The first printers on the market were from Qume and Genicom, both of which released models in late 1985. Today, there are dozens of compatible printers on the market, with prices ranging from below $1,500 to well over $10,000.

This chapter takes a quick look at a few compatibles. It is not intended to be comprehensive but simply to give you a sense of the range of options available on printers made by manufacturers other than Hewlett-Packard.

PRINTER ENGINES

A laser printer contains two main components: the printer engine and the controller.

The **printer engine** is the physical machinery — the hardware. Canon's engine was used in the first LaserJet, Apple's original LaserWriter, and all other first-generation laser printers. Today, Canon faces stiff competition from such manufacturers as Epson, Kyocera, Hitachi, Ricoh, Toshiba, and others.

As you can see from Figure 13.1, the printer engine makes a big difference in the overall life of your printer — particularly if you will be using it in a very busy office. In such an environment, printer speed and long-term life can be quite important. For example, if you plan to produce 1.5 million pages in the next two or three years, the extra money spent on a machine built around Ricoh's heavy-duty 4150 engine, for example, might be a far better deal than the cost of the five Kyocera F2010-based printers it would take to replace it.

Laser Printer Engines			
Manufacturer	Model	Life (thousands of pages)	Pages/min
Kyocera	1000A	600	10
Kyocera	F3010	—	18
Kyocera	F2010	300	10
Ricoh	4060	180	6
Ricoh	4081	600	8
Ricoh	4150	1,500	15
Canon	LBP-CX	100	8
Canon	LBP-CXD	200	8
Toshiba		600	12

Figure 13.1   Laser Printer Engines

THE CONTROLLER BOARD

The other main printer component is the **controller** — the internal computer that tells the printer engine what to do. The controller is what makes an Apple LaserWriter completely different from a LaserJet, despite the fact that each uses the same engine.

Many printers can emulate the LaserJet+ because their controller boards are designed to respond to the same commands in the same ways.

MARKET DIFFERENTIATION

To help their products stand out in the marketplace, most manufacturers of LaserJet compatibles throw in various extras, such as more built-in fonts, the ability to respond to other printer commands, or a better printer engine. These companies hope to lure you away from the safe, secure choice of Hewlett-Packard. As a result, many of the compatibles do more for less money than do Hewlett-Packard printers.

The best place for up-to-date printer information is probably *PC Magazine*'s annual printer review issue, published each November. The 1987 printer review issue examined three dozen laser printers from 26 different manufacturers; three years earlier, the roundup included only one laser printer — the original LaserJet. In the 1987 review, two-thirds of the reviewed printers claimed LaserJet+ compatibility; their prices ranged from $1,795 to a hefty $18,750. The latest Hewlett-Packard offering — the LaserJet Series II — lists for $2,495 (though it can often be purchased for much less).

THE MANNESMANN TALLY MT910

Mannesmann Tally is a name better known in the industrial printer market than in the consumer printer field. The company — a subsidiary of a German industrial giant — specialized for many years in custom printer orders for large corporations.

The company entered the consumer printer market in 1984 with a few dot matrix models. The results were encouraging, so they continue to expand their presence in the consumer market in addition to filling custom orders.

The MT910 laser printer is Mannesmann Tally's first venture into the laser printer field. The MT910 is built around a Kyocera printer engine and has a life expectancy of 600,000 pages. The Canon engines at the core of the Hewlett-Packard machines use a single cartridge that contains toner and all the printer's replaceable parts. The Kyocera engine handles each of those elements separately. As a result, more items need changing, but each item is changed only when necessary — not every time you run out of toner.

Other Emulations

In addition to emulating the HP LaserJet+, the MT910 can also emulate an Epson FX-80, an IBM Proprinter, a Qume Sprint 11, or a Diablo 630. You cannot use software commands to switch emulations on the fly; you must use a set of switches on the printer's front panel to change emulations.

MT Superset

One of the better features of the MT910 is a command language referred to as the MT Superset — which is made up of commands that are active no matter which emulation you are using. The commands are very similar to those in Hewlett-Packard's Printer Control Language. For example, if you were working with older software that would only work with the Diablo 630 emulation, you would not normally be able to change fonts; the Diablo printer is a daisy wheel printer that can only switch fonts if you stop it and change print wheels. Using the MT Superset, however, you can change to any of the resident or downloaded fonts loaded in the printer, just as you could in LaserJet+ mode.

LaserJet Overrides

The MT910 can also override some of the LaserJet+'s limitations. For example, to use a landscape, italic, or bold font on the LaserJet+, you need a separate font with that trait. When you ask the MT910 for a font with one of those traits, it first searches to see if one is available. If it is not, the printer will either rotate, slant, or darken a font as instructed.

The MT910 can also reverse a font (white characters on a black background), and it automatically supports 14 symbol sets, without requiring separate fonts.

Other valuable features of the MT910 include the ability to rotate fonts without rotating the page. For example, if you are trying to print pages that will eventually be cut in half and bound, you may need part of the page printed upside down. The MT910 can print pages upside down or rotated 90 degrees right or left. If you need larger fonts than the printer normally supports, you can achieve them with font-scaling commands that can produce characters as high as 450 points (6.25").

If you must work in an emulation other than the LaserJet+, the MT910 can still work with its own variety of macros, making complicated printing chores easy — even chores normally beyond the capability of the printer being emulated.

For More Information

Mannesmann-Tally Corporation
8301 South 180th Street
Kent, WA 98032
(206) 251-5500

OASYS

OASYS (Office Automation SYStems, Inc.) is an example of another type of company that has moved into the laser printer market. Unlike Mannesmann-Tally, OASYS is a small company that began with the idea of building a better laser printer. To a large degree they have succeeded, currently producing a line of six different laser printers at prices as low as $2,300. All OASYS printers are built around sturdy Ricoh printer engines with engine lives as high as 1.5 million copies. OASYS printers feature at least 19 built-in fonts (often more) and emulate Epson, Diablo, NEC, and IBM printers in addition to the LaserJet+.

Two features that help make the OASYS printers stand out from the crowd are the Express Command Language and the Pyramid Font System. (These features are not available on all OASYS printers, so check to see if the model you are looking at includes them.)

Express

Express is a simple page-description language — a programming language that allows you to control a printer with simple commands. With OASYS printers, you can embed Express commands in the text by using the character sequence (O]. The printer then interprets everything after that sequence — until it comes to the expression EXIT — as part of a program.

For example, on an OASYS printer with Express, the command

```
(O] CIR 1.5; EXIT;
```

will draw a circle 1.5" in diameter, centered on the print position at the time the printer received the initial parenthesis of the (O] sequence.

You can use Express to change fonts; move around the page; draw circles, pie charts, boxes, and bars (with various fill patterns); and print bar codes.

Pyramid Font System

Even the most inexpensive OASYS printer comes with many fonts (19), but the better ones contain the Pyramid font system, which easily and quickly gives you a wide variety of fonts. The system uses commands in the Express language to generate fonts from mathematical models stored in the printer's permanent memory. So if you want a Times Roman font that is 20 points high, slanted 20 degrees to the right, hollow centered, 20% bolded horizontally, 10% bolded vertically, and rotated 90 degrees left, the printer will create that font for you.

The problem with printer-generated fonts is that the software you are using does not always know the width of the characters, which means it is hard to use printer-generated proportional fonts with software that expects to know the character widths. In spite of that limitation, however, the Pyramid font system is a worthwhile addition to a LaserJet+ compatible printer.

For More Information

Office Automation Systems, Inc.
8352 Clairmont Mesa Blvd.
San Diego, CA 92111
(619) 576-9500

CIE TERMINAL LIPS 10 PLUS

CIE Terminals' LIPS laser printer is actually an OASYS controller board in a Konica print engine with a CIE Terminals label on the outside. As a result, the LIPS printers are almost identical in performance to the OASYS machines. The main distinguishing factors are capital cost and the cost of operation.

A distinct advantage of the CIE printer over comparable OASYS models is the front panel operation. OASYS requires that you print a status sheet to determine how your printer is configured. CIE gives you all the necessary information on a small digital readout in English — not in arcane codes such as ERR: 10B.

For More Information

CIE Terminals Inc.
2505 McCabe Way
Irvine, CA 92714-6297
(714) 660-1441

THE LIMITS OF EMULATION

Not all printers that claim to be LaserJet+ compatible actually are compatible. Several printers that claim compatibility work properly most of the time, but they might give you problems now and then. Before you purchase a LaserJet+ compatible printer, get a guarantee (in writing) from your dealer that the printer is 100% compatible or get some type of listing describing exactly how it differs from the LaserJet+.

Compatibles and Fonts

Two of the most common printing problems involve font cartridges in compatibles. Most compatibles do not use Hewlett-Packard font cartridges. Naturally, the manufacturers want you to buy font cartridges from them; however, on these cartridges, the selection of fonts is usually a bit different from the Hewlett-Packard models, and, even on seemingly identical cartridges, font widths often differ.

The fact that different selections of fonts are available becomes a problem when you install various software packages for your printer. Normally, when asked what printer you have, you would indicate that you have a Hewlett-Packard LaserJet+. Many programs ask you what font cartridge you have and make assumptions about what fonts are available, based on the information you provide. For example, if you have a cartridge containing a 10-point Times Roman font, you may instruct a program that you have the Hewlett-Packard F font cartridge. The F font cartridge, however, also contains 14-point Helvetica bold and 8-point Times Roman fonts. If your cartridge does not contain these fonts, the program may not always give you the fonts you want. The only solution is to manually modify the printer drivers for that program if possible, perhaps through your word processing program (see Chapters 14 and 15).

Width Tables

The second common printing problem is minor but can be very irritating if you want to align text. This is a problem with font character widths of cartridge fonts. On many of the compatibles, the characters on the cartridges are not quite the same width as those on the Hewlett-Packard cartridges. Again, the program may be expecting a certain collection of fonts at certain widths. Because your cartridge widths are different, your output may not look the way you expected.

That's why it might make more sense to use soft fonts when working on a compatible, unless you know that the character widths of the cartridge font you will be using are the same as those on Hewlett-Packard cartridges.

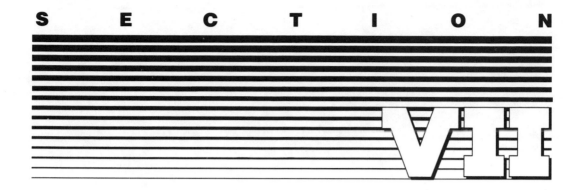

THE LASERJET + AND SOFTWARE

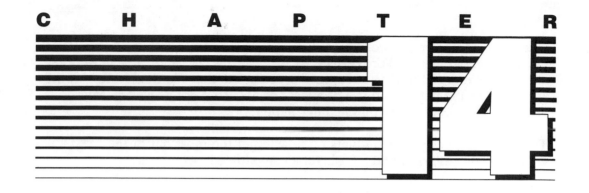

C H A P T E R

14

USING THE
LASERJET + WITH WORDPERFECT

One of the most popular word processing programs available today for the IBM PC and compatibles is WordPerfect. It is powerful, fast, and capable of doing almost anything you might want a word processor to do. WordPerfect's abilities are fairly well matched to those of a laser printer (but not as well as Microsoft Word's abilities, which are outlined in Chapter 15).

This chapter gives you some hints on how to get the most out of the MS-DOS version of WordPerfect and a LaserJet+ compatible laser printer.

This chapter covers the following topics:

- WordPerfect printer drivers
- Changing fonts in WordPerfect
- Taking direct control of the printer
- Printing an envelope with WordPerfect
- Modifying a printer driver
- Customizing your own printer driver

The material in this chapter applies to WordPerfect version 4.2, the WordPerfect Printer program version 4.5, and the WordPerfect printer Help program version 1.0.

WORDPERFECT PRINTER DRIVERS

WordPerfect Corporation provides dozens of printer drivers to support its software. A printer driver contains the information WordPerfect needs to access the special features of a printer, such as the command to turn underlining on or off.

WordPerfect's printer drivers are found in files on the WordPerfect distribution disks labelled "Printer 1" and "Printer 2." A file named WPRINT1.ALL on the Printer 1 disk contains most of the printer drivers. There are more drivers on the Printer 2 disk in a file named WPRINT2.ALL. Together, the two disks contain over a hundred printer drivers. WPRINT1.ALL contains the drivers for the HP LaserJet.

There are so many LaserJet drivers because each driver supports only a few of the many fonts available on cartridges and disks for a LaserJet+. WordPerfect can only support eight fonts in each printer driver. If a printer driver doesn't exist for the combination of fonts you are using, you can create your own, using the WordPerfect Printer program.

Finding the Drivers You Need

The first thing you must do is find the printer drivers you need. Use WordPerfect's Printer Help program to determine what fonts and special effects each printer driver supports.

To start the Printer Help program, insert the disk containing the program PRHELP.EXE or, if you are using a hard disk, change to the directory containing the program. (On WordPerfect distribution disks, PRHELP.EXE is on the disk labeled "Printer 2.") At the DOS prompt, enter

```
PRHELP [Return]
```

When the Printer Help program loads, it will list the printer drivers available with your version of WordPerfect. The listing continues for several screens. Press the [PgDn] key until you see the screen listing the LaserJet printer drivers.

Place the cursor over the first LaserJet driver, HP LaserJet A, and press the [Return] key. The program will display a Help screen for that printer driver. The screen will display the name of the driver, information about which fonts and special features it supports, and notes about how to modify the print driver for other related fonts. Examine the driver named "HP LaserJet Soft AA Times Roman," which you will use later in an example.

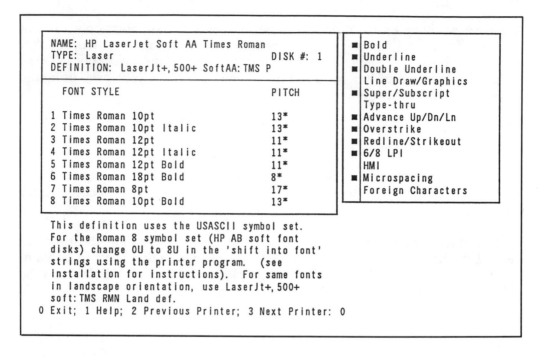

```
  NAME: HP LaserJet Soft AA Times Roman          ■ Bold
  TYPE: Laser                        DISK #: 1    ■ Underline
  DEFINITION: LaserJt+, 500+ SoftAA: TMS P        ■ Double Underline
                                                    Line Draw/Graphics
     FONT STYLE                       PITCH       ■ Super/Subscript
                                                    Type-thru
  1 Times Roman 10pt                   13*        ■ Advance Up/Dn/Ln
  2 Times Roman 10pt Italic            13*        ■ Overstrike
  3 Times Roman 12pt                   11*        ■ Redline/Strikeout
  4 Times Roman 12pt Italic            11*        ■ 6/8 LPI
  5 Times Roman 12pt Bold              11*          HMI
  6 Times Roman 18pt Bold               8*        ■ Microspacing
  7 Times Roman 8pt                    17*          Foreign Characters
  8 Times Roman 10pt Bold              13*

     This definition uses the USASCII symbol set.
     For the Roman 8 symbol set (HP AB soft font
     disks) change 0U to 8U in the 'shift into font'
     strings using the printer program. (see
     installation for instructions). For same fonts
     in landscape orientation, use LaserJt+, 500+
     soft:TMS RMN Land def.
   0 Exit; 1 Help; 2 Previous Printer; 3 Next Printer: 0
```

Figure 14.1   *WordPerfect's Printer Driver Help Screen*

While examining the details of any LaserJet driver, you can scroll through the other entries by pressing [3] to move to the next entry in the list or [2] to move back to the previous entry on the list.

After finding the right drivers for the jobs and fonts you have, write down their names. If you can't find the exact driver you need, write the name of a driver that most closely matches your requirements. You will learn to customize drivers later in this chapter.

Also, for future reference, list the fonts and pitches supported by the printer drivers you want.

To exit the WordPerfect Printer Help program, press [0].

Selecting Printer Drivers

Next, you must use WordPerfect to select printers. You can assign a particular printer driver to a printer number between 1 and 6. Then, you can change printer drivers easily by simply changing printer numbers.

Put your working copy of WordPerfect in drive A and your Printer 1 disk in drive B. If you have a hard disk system, change to the directory containing your Word-Perfect program files and the files WPRINT1.ALL and WPRINT2.ALL. If you are not sure how to change directories, see your DOS manual.

Start WordPerfect by entering

```
WP [Return]
```

If this is the first time you have loaded WordPerfect, the program will display a Help screen that will not appear after you have selected printers. If you have pre-viousy loaded WordPerfect, you will see the standard WordPerfect edit screen.

Press [Shift/F7]. The Print Menu will appear at the bottom of the screen.

```
1 Full Text; 2 Page; 3 Options; 4 Printer Control; 5 Type-thru; 6 Preview: 0
```

Press [4] to go to the WordPerfect Printer Control menu.

```
         Printer Control
                                 C - Cancel Print Job(s)
         1 - Select Print Options     D - Display All Print Jobs
         2 - Display Printers and Fonts  G - "Go" (Resume Printing)
         3 - Select Printers          P - Print a Document
                                 R - Rush Print Job
         Selection: 0             S - Stop Printing


         Current Job

         Job Number: n/a            Page Number:  n/a
         Job Status: n/a            Current Copy: n/a
         Message:    The print queue is empty

         Job List

         Job  Document        Destination      Forms and Print Options


         Additional jobs not shown: 0
```

Figure 14.2   *The WordPerfect Printer Control Menu*

Next, press [3] to see the Select Printers menu.

```
    Printer Definitions in C:\WORDPERF\WPRINTER.FIL

       1  Standard Printer        2  DOS Text Printer
       3  TI 855 - Custom         4  TmsRmn/Helvet - Letter
       5  TmsRmn 10 / Helv        6  LaserJet T: Helv Tax
       7  MT910 - Courier         8  LaserJt Reg,+,500+ A: Courier




                                  PgDn for Additional Printer Definitions
                                  Exit when Done
    Printer 1                     Cancel to Ignore Changes
    Using Definition: 5           Arrow Keys to Change Printer Number
```

Figure 14.3   *The Select Printers Menu*

At the top of the screen, you will see a list of the printer drivers in a file called WPRINTER.FIL, which should be in your WordPerfect directory or on the disk in drive A. These printer drivers are immediately available to Word-Perfect. (Note that your list will differ from the one in Figure 14.3.)

Examine the lower left corner of the screen. The cursor should be under the number after the words "Using Definition." This is the number of the printer definition currently assigned to printer number 1. You can change that number to correspond to any of the printer drivers on your screen.

The printer driver you selected with the WordPerfect Printer Help program is probably not listed. Press [PgDn]. WordPerfect will then search the WPRINT1.ALL file for other printer drivers and begin listing them on the screen. Continue pressing [PgDn] until you see the listing of HP LaserJet printer drivers.

```
Printer Definitions in WPRINT1.ALL

  97  LaserJt Reg,+,500+ J: Math E    98  LaserJt Reg,+,500+ L: Cou P&L
  99  LaserJt Reg,+,500+ M: P E P&L  100  LaserJt Reg,+,500+ N: L G P&L
 101  LaserJt Reg,+,500+ Q: Cour,LG  102  LaserJt Reg,+,500+ R: Present
 103  LaserJt Reg,+,500+ W: BarCode  104  LaserJt Reg,+,500+ Y: PC Cour
 105  LaserJt+,500+ B: Tms Rmn 1     106  LaserJt+,500+ F: Tms Rmn 2
 107  LaserJt+,500+ K: Tms Rmn Math  108  LaserJt+,500+ P: Tms Rmn P&L
 109  LaserJt+,500+ Soft AA: Helv L  110  LaserJt+,500+ Soft AA: Helv P
 111  LaserJt+,500+ Soft AA: Tm/Hel  112  LaserJt+,500+ Soft AA: Tms L
 113  LaserJt+,500+ Soft AA: Tms P   114  LaserJt+,500+ Soft AC: Helv P
 115  LaserJt+,500+ Soft AC: Tms P   116  LaserJt+,500+ Soft AE: Helv P
 117  LaserJt+,500+ Soft AE: Tms P   118  LaserJt+,500+ Soft DA: LG,Prs
 119  LaserJt+,500+ Soft EA: PElite  120  LaserJt+,500+ T: Helv Tax
 121  LaserJt+,500+ U: Forms Port    122  LaserJt+,500+ V: Forms Land
 123  LaserWriter Helv Landscape     124  LaserWriter Helv Portrait
 125  LaserWriter Times Landscape    126  LaserWriter Times Portrait
 127  MPI Printmate 150              128  Mannesmann Tally MT180


                                     PgDn for Additional Printer Definitions
                                     Exit when Done
Printer 6                            Cancel to Ignore Changes
Using Definition:                    Arrow Keys to Change Printer Number
```

Figure 14.4   *Listing of Hewlett-Packard LaserJet Printer Drivers*

If you add the HP drivers to WPRINTER.FIL, they will appear on the screen every time you choose the Select Printers option from the Printer Control screen. To add them to the WPRINTER.FIL file, you must temporarily assign them to a printer.

Adding Printer Drivers

The cursor should still be in the lower left corner of your screen, where you will see the following:

```
Printer 1
Using Definition: _
```

Type the number of the printer you want to add to the WPRINTER.FIL file, and press [Return].

The next screen will ask you for a "Printer Port"—the port through which your computer sends data to the printer.

```
Printer Port
     0 - LPT 1     1 - LPT 2     2 - LPT 3
     4 - COM 1     5 - COM 2     6 - COM 3     7 - COM 4
     8 - Device or File Pathname
Selection: _
```

Figure 14.5   *The Printer Port Menu*

There are two types of printer interface ports: parallel and serial. A **parallel port** uses eight wires to send eight bits of data to the printer at the same time, like eight people walking side by side and reaching the same destination simultaneously. A **serial port** uses one wire and sends the data one bit at a time, like eight people walking single file. To find out which kind of printer port(s) your computer and printer has, consult the manuals that came with those units. If your printer has a parallel interface, you should probably select LPT1, which means Line Printer port #1 (or parallel port #1). If you plan to use more than one printer, one of them can be connected to LPT2 or LPT3.

Ports labeled COM1 through COM4 are serial ports. If your printer has an RS-232-C or RS-422 serial interface, select the appropriate serial port. When you select a serial port, WordPerfect asks you to select the appropriate baud rate, parity, and protocol.

```
Baud Select
       0 -   110     1 -   150     2 -   300     3 -   600
       4 -  1200     5 -  2400     6 -  4800     7 -  9600
Selection: 4

Parity
       0 - None      1 - Odd       3 - Even
Selection: 3

Stop Bits (1 or 2): 1
Character Length (7 or 8): 7
```

Figure 14.6   *Serial Port Parameters Menu*

It does not matter what the serial port parameters are, as long as they are the same for the printer and WordPerfect. If the parameters are not the same, the printer and computer will not know how to communicate. Also, though you can set the printer and computer to communicate as slowly as 110 bits per second, it is usually not a good idea to do so. Most LaserJet+ compatible printers can print 8-18 pages per minute. A page can contain up to about 12,000 characters, so setting the speed to 110 bits per second could slow your printer to as little as one page every 18 minutes. The best bet is to set the transmission rate as high as possible.

Type of Forms

Finally, after selecting the printer port, you will be asked to select the "Type of Forms." The program must know how paper is fed into your printer.

```
Type of Forms
     1 - Continuous
     2 - Hand Fed
     3 - Sheet Feeder
Selection: 1
```

Figure 14.7   *Type of Forms Menu*

Experiment with these settings. On some printers, if you select 1 (Continuous), the printer will operate at maximum speed, but it will only use paper from one of two available paper cassettes. If you choose 3 (Sheet Feeder), you will be able to use WordPerfect to switch paper cassettes but, due to the interaction of the printer and the software, the printer speed may be reduced by 50%.

For now, define one printer as using Continuous and define another as using Sheet Feeder. Try them both to see which works best for you.

Sheet Feeder Definitions

If your printer has more than one paper-feed tray, and you have defined a printer as using a sheet feeder, select 3 to assign a sheet feeder to this printer definition. When you press [Return], you will see the Sheet Feeder Information menu.

```
Sheet Feeder Information
        Number of Extra Lines Between Pages (12 LPI):  24
        Column Position of Left Edge of Paper (10 Pitch):  0
        Number of Sheet Feeder Bins (1-7):  3
```

Figure 14.8   Sheet Feeder Information Menu

You may need to experiment with these settings for them to work correctly with your printer.

Press [Return] for the first item (Number of Extra Lines Between Pages). Define the second item (Column Position of Left Edge of Paper) with 0. The number of sheet feeder bins is two or three; count one for each physical paper cassette your printer has and one for the manual feed slot. On most printers, Number 1 is the top cassette, number 2 is the bottom cassette, and number 3 is the manual feed tray.

Next, you will be asked for the sheet feeder type.

```
┌─────────────────────────────────────────────────────────────────┐
│                                                                   │
│                                                                   │
│  Sheet Feeder Type                                                │
│                                                                   │
│     1 HP LaserJet                           2 HP LaserJet 500+    │
│                                                                   │
│                                                                   │
│                                                                   │
└─────────────────────────────────────────────────────────────────┘
```

Figure 14.9   Sheet Feeder Type Menu

Enter the number next to "HP LaserJet" if your printer has only one paper cassette or the number next to "HP LaserJet 500+" if you have more than one paper cassette. Then, press [Return].

When you have selected the printer drivers you need, return to the Printer Control screen by pressing [F7]—the Exit key. Press [Return] to return to the WordPerfect edit screen. The printer drivers you selected should have been added to your WPRINTER.FIL. The next time you go to the Select Printers screen, they will be listed among the choices.

Finally, leave WordPerfect by again pressing [F7] and then [N] and [Y]. You should return to the DOS prompt.

CHANGING FONTS IN WORDPERFECT

Once you have selected a printer driver, changing fonts in WordPerfect is easy. When you used the Printer Help program, you were asked to list the fonts and pitches supported by each printer driver selected. Now, you will use that information.

To change fonts while running WordPerfect, press [CTRL/F8], which takes you to WordPerfect's Print Format menu.

```
Print Format

        1 - Pitch                      14*
            Font                        1

        2 - Lines per Inch              6

    Right Justification                Off
        3 - Turn off
        4 - Turn on

    Underline Style                     6
        5 - Non-continuous Single
        6 - Non-continuous Double
        7 - Continuous Single
        8 - Continuous Double

        9 - Sheet Feeder Bin Number     1

        A - Insert Printer Command

        B - Line Numbering             Off

    Selection: 0
```

Figure 14.10   Print Format Menu

Press [1]; the cursor will jump to the top of the right column, under the number for pitch. Enter the value for the new font's pitch, and then enter its font number. Consider an example. Earlier, you used the Printer Help program to examine a printer driver called "HP LaserJet Soft AA Times Roman," which indicated that the eight fonts supported by this driver and their recommended pitches are as follows (see Figure 14.11):

Number	Name	Pitch
1	Times Roman 10pt	13*
2	Times Roman 10pt Italic	13*
3	Times Roman 12pt	11*
4	Times Roman 12pt Italic	11*
5	Times Roman 12pt Bold	11*
6	Times Roman 18pt Bold	8*
7	Times Roman 8pt	17*
8	Times Roman 10pt Bold	13*

Figure 14.11   Example Driver's Fonts and Recommended Pitches

The asterisks inform WordPerfect that these fonts are proportionally spaced.

To switch to Times Roman 18-point bold type, enter a pitch of 8* and a font number of 6, as follows

```
Print Format

     1 - Pitch              8*
         Font               6
```

To switch to Times Roman 10-point Italic, use a pitch of 13* and a font number of 2, as follows

```
Print Format

     1 - Pitch              13*
         Font               2
```

TAKING DIRECT CONTROL OF THE PRINTER

Occasionally, you must switch to a font not supported by the printer driver you are using. You then must give the instructions to send that font directly to the printer, using WordPerfect's Insert Printer Command function.

Perform this task from the Print Format screen — the same screen used to select fonts in the conventional way. This time, however, select A (for Insert Printer Command). At the bottom of the Print Format screen, WordPerfect will print

```
Cmnd: _
```

with the cursor just beyond the colon. You can now enter the command to select a font or perform any other printer function, such as changing orientations, rotating a font, drawing a box by using LaserJet block and pattern graphics, or whatever else you need to do.

You enter control characters such as <u>ESC</u> by typing their ASCII number between angle brackets. For example, to send <u>ESC</u> to the printer, enter <27> after the **Cmnd:** prompt as follows:

```
<27>
```

To switch to landscape orientation for a page, enter

```
<27>&l1O
```

which is the command for landscape orientation on a LaserJet+.

Note that there are no spaces between the characters in the command string. Even though there are spaces in the commands listed in this book, they are there only to make the commands easier to read. Do not enter those spaces when sending the commands to the printer.

You can use WordPerfect's ability to directly control the printer to give it any commands the printer driver cannot.

PRINTING AN ENVELOPE WITH WORDPERFECT

One of the most difficult tasks to perform with most printers is addressing an envelope, but this task can be accomplished using WordPerfect and a LaserJet+ compatible printer.

First, start WordPerfect or exit any file on which you may be working. Now, with a clear WordPerfect screen, you are ready to create a file for addressing your envelopes. You must format a page for the envelope's odd shape and then switch to a landscape font and the manual feed tray.

Landscape Font

You must first determine whether or not your printer has an appropriate landscape font. Basic LaserJets and LaserJet+ models have only one internal landscape font—a tiny line printer font, which is not really appropriate for addressing an envelope. The LaserJet Series II—and almost all compatible printers—include at least a resident landscape Courier font. Other printers can rotate any font to landscape orientation. Try using the LaserJet A printer driver, which contains the information needed to use a landscape Courier font.

Press [Ctrl/F7] for the Print Format menu. Option number 9 selects a sheet feeder bin (paper cassette).

```
9 - Sheet Feeder Bin Number     3
```

On most LaserJet+ compatibles, sheet feeder bin #3 is the manual feed tray. Press [9], [3], and [Return] to select the manual feed tray.

Next, without leaving the Print Format screen, select font 4.

```
1 - Pitch                  10
    Font                    4
```

In the LaserJet+ Courier printer driver, font 4 is the landscape Courier font you want for printing envelopes. Press [Return] to return to the edit screen.

Adjusting the Margins

Next, you must adjust the margins because an envelope's shape differs from that of a piece of paper, and some printers assume manually fed paper is a different size.

To set the top margin, press [Alt/F8] for the Page Format menu.

```
Page Format

        1 - Page Number Position

        2 - New Page Number

        3 - Center Page Top to Bottom

        4 - Page Length

        5 - Top Margin

        6 - Headers or Footers

        7 - Page Number Column Positions

        8 - Suppress for Current page only

        9 - Conditional End of Page

        A - Widow/Orphan

    Selection: 0
```

Figure 14.12   *Page Format Menu*

Item 5 sets the top margin. Set the value to 30 half-lines (30 half-lines = 15 lines = 2.5").

Next, press [Shift/F8] to see the Line Format menu at the bottom of the screen.

```
1 2 Tabs; 3 Margins; 4 Spacing; 5 Hyphenation; 6 Align Char: 0
```

Set the side margins to Left=50 and Right=160. (You may need to experiment with these settings, depending on how your printer deals with paper in the manual feed slot.)

Inserting the Address

Next, enter your return address. Then, space down four lines and reset the side margins to Left=80 and Right=160. Enter

```
Address Here.
```

Save the file under the name ENVELOPE on your WordPerfect working disk or in the WordPerfect directory on your hard drive.

Printing the Envelope File

To print an envelope, you must use the LaserJet A printer driver. Press [Shift/F7] to access the Print menu and [4] for the Printer Control screen. Press [2] to see the names of the printer drivers you have assigned to the six printers you can use with WordPerfect. If "HP LaserJet A (Courier 10)" is not one of the names, use the Select Printers procedure outlined earlier in this chapter to select it.

Now that you know the number of the printer to which the LaserJetA printer driver is assigned, press [Return] until you return to the edit screen. Press [Shift/F7] again, but this time, press [3] for Options. You will be given a chance to assign a printer driver for a single printing.

```
Change Print Options Temporarily

    1 - Printer Number            1

    2 - Number of Copies          1

    3 - Binding Width (1/10 in.)   0
```

Assign the printer, using the LaserJet A printer driver. When you finish selecting the printer, you will return to the Printer menu. Press [1] to print the file; remember, feed an envelope into the manual-feed tray.

MODIFYING WORDPERFECT PRINTER DRIVERS

The WordPerfect Printer program allows you to modify almost all features of a WordPerfect printer driver. The Printer program allows you to manipulate, edit, and create printer drivers. Study the manual for WordPerfect's printer program carefully before attempting to modify any WordPerfect printer driver.

Floppy Disk Start Up

If you are using a floppy disk system, insert your working copy of the WordPerfect program disk with the file PRINTER.EXE in drive B and the disk with the file WPRINTER.FIL in drive A. Make sure you are logged on to drive A. The prompt should be as follows:

```
A:>
```

or

```
A:\>
```

Start the Printer program by entering

```
B:PRINTER [Return]
```

Hard Disk Start Up

If you are using a hard disk system, change to the directory containing WFRINTER.FIL and PRINTER.EXE. Start the program by entering

```
PRINTER [Return]
```

The Printer Main Menu

When the printer program loads, it will display a menu offering six choices.

```
  PRINTER:  WordPerfect Printer Definition Program

Please Choose One:

    1. General Information and Help

    2. Explanation of Special Codes Used in This Program

    3. Printer Definitions (Examine, Change)

    4. Character Tables (Examine, Change)

    5. Sheet Feeder Definitions (Examine, Change)

    0. Exit

Selection: 0
```

Figure 14.13   Printer Main Menu

Option 1 explains the operation of the Printer program. Option 2 explains the meaning of some special codes used in the Printer program. Both of these topics are covered thoroughly in the manual for the Printer program that comes with your WordPerfect software.

Select Option 3. At the bottom of the screen, you will see a list of all printer drivers in your WPRINTER.FIL. (Note that your list will differ from the example in this book.)

```
                        Printers Currently Defined

    1  Standard Printer              2  DOS Text Printer
    3  TI 855 - Custom               4  TmsRmn/Helvet - Letter
    5  TmsRmn 10 / Helv              6  LaserJet T: Helv Tax
    7  MT910 - Courier               8  LaserJt Reg,+,500+ A: Courier
    9  LaserJt+,500+ Soft AA: Tms P
```

Figure 14.14   *WPRINTER.FIL Printer Drivers*

Editing a Printer Driver

Often, you must make a minor change to a printer driver. For example, you may have chosen the Hewlett-Packard LaserJet+ T (Helv. Tax) driver, which is a driver designed to work with the Helvetica-like fonts found on Hewlett-Packard's T font cartridge. The fonts on this cartridge use the USASCII symbol set. Similar soft fonts are available from Hewlett-Packard, but these fonts use the Roman-8 symbol set, which means that to use this printer driver for the soft fonts, you need a font selection escape sequence that begins

<u>ESC</u> (8U

The printer driver, however, will use an escape sequence that begins

<u>ESC</u> (0U

Press [B] to edit a printer definition. When the program asks you which printer to edit, enter the number of the HP LaserJet+ T (Helv. Tax) driver.

The next screen offers you a 10-item menu.

```
              Edit:        LaserJet T: Helv Tax

    1. Printer Initialization

    2. Carriage Return/Backspace Control

    3. Line Spacing and Vertical Motion Control (VMI)

    4. Microspacing and Horizontal Motion Control (HMI)

    5. Subscript/Superscript/Underline/Bold

    6. Special Text Markings

    7. Pitch/Miscellaneous

    8. Selecting Fonts (Fonts 1 - 4)

    9. Selecting Fonts (Fonts 5 - 8)

    A. Character Tables for Fonts



    Select Item Number: 0
```

Figure 14.15   *Hewlett-Packard LaserJet+ T-Driver Edit Menu*

Selecting Font Commands

You are interested in items 8 and 9, which are the commands for selecting fonts. Press 8; you will see the commands for fonts 1 through 4.

```
    Edit: LaserJet T: Helv Tax      Changing Fonts (#'s 1-4)

1. Shift Into Font 1
   <27>(0U<27>(s1p10vs1b4T<M>
2. Shift Out of Font 1

3. Shift Into Font 2
   <27>(0U<27>(s1p12vs1b4T<M>
4. Shift Out of Font 2

5. Shift Into Font 3
   <27>(0U<27>(s1p14vs1b4T<M>
6. Shift Out of Font 3

7. Shift Into Font 4
   <27>(0U<27>(s1p8vs1b4T<M>
8. Shift Out of Font 4
```

Figure 14.16   Commands for Hewlett-Packard LaserJet+ T Fonts 1-4

Note that each command begins with

```
<27>(0U
```

<27> stands for ESC, and the command ESC (0U selects a font with the USASCII symbol set.

If you change each of those commands so it begins

```
<27>(8U
```

you will be asking for a font with the Roman-8 symbol set, which is the symbol set for the soft fonts. Select each of the font selection sequences in turn and change the 0U to 8U.

This type of minor change to the font selection commands is probably all you will ever need to do with the WordPerfect Printer program.

CUSTOMIZING YOUR OWN PRINTER DRIVER

Occasionally, however, you may need your own printer driver for a special project. For example, you might want a driver that includes a combination of Times Roman and Letter Gothic fonts. Because none of the drivers distributed with WordPerfect includes that particular combination of fonts, you must create your own driver.

Start at the Printers Currently Defined screen, but select A from the menu to create a new printer driver. The Printer program then asks for a New Printer Name. **Tip:** start your new name with a space or it will not line up with the other printer drivers on the menu.

The next request is for Current Printer to Use as a Pattern. When you select this pattern driver, the Printer program copies the driver into a new driver under the name you have selected. You can then edit that driver, making the changes you need to produce the printer driver you want.

For this example, start with the HP LaserJet+ P (Tms Rmn P&L) driver. "P&L" indicate that this driver supports both Portrait and Landscape fonts. For most purposes, however, you won't need any landscape fonts. Replace the commands for selecting fonts 5 through 8 in the original driver with commands for selecting the Letter Gothic fonts you need. Because Letter Gothic is a fixed-space font, you needn't worry about a width table for it.

For proportionally spaced fonts, you must select the appropriate character table. First, choose item A, "Character Tables for Fonts," from the printer driver edit screen. Doing so will take you to the screen for selecting width tables (see Figure 14.17). This screen lists a width table for each font in the driver you are editing.

```
      1. Character Table for Font 1
         Courier    12
      2. Character Table for Font 2
         LinePr     8
      3. Character Table for Font 3
         optima 6
      4. Character Table for Font 4
         Optima 8
      5. Character Table for Font 5
         Cent.School.14B
      6. Character Table for Font 6
         Cent.School.18B
      7. Character Table for Font 7

      8. Character Table for Font 8

      9. Examine or Edit a Character Table




      Select Item Number: 0
```

Figure 14.17   Character Width Tables for Fonts

Press the number of the font for which you want to change the width table. The program will display a list of the available width tables. These are the width tables for all the fonts in all the drivers in WPRINTER.FIL.

```
            Edit:      HP LaserJet+ Compatible
       Edit Character Tables


        1 Standard ASCII     2 Extended ASCII     3 ASCII/Backspace    4 ASCII/Line Ptr
        5 Prestige 12        6 LsrJt Romn 10      7 LsrJt-F Italic     8 LsrJt-F Bold
        9 LsrJt Helv 10     10 LsrJt Helv 12     11 LsrJt Helv 14     12 LsrJt Helv8 B
       13 LsrJt Helv8 N     14 LsrJt Helv 6      15 Helv       24B    16 LaserJet Rmn 8
       17 LaserJet+ Graph   18 LaserJet+ Box     19 LaserJet- Box     20 Courier    12
       21 Helv         6    22 Helv         8    23 Unknown      9    24 Unknown     14
       25 LinePr       8    26 optima 6          27 Optima 8         28 Cent.School.14B
       29 Cent.School.18B   30 HP Soft Tms 10N   31 HP Soft Tms 10I   32 HP Soft Tms 12N
       33 HP Soft Tms 12I   34 HP Soft Tms 12B   35 HP Soft Tms 18B   36 HP Soft Tms 8N
       37 HP Soft Tms 10B




       Select Character Table for Font: _
```

Figure 14.18   Width Tables for WPRINTER.FIL Driver Fonts

Enter the number of the width table you want and press [Return].

WordPerfect and Soft Fonts

To use WordPerfect with soft fonts for which there are no printer drivers, use a font manager program such as the Conofont Manager from Conographic Corporation, the WordPerfect Font Manager from SWFTE International, or the MSWP program from VS Software. These programs can read a font file and create a WordPerfect printer driver for that font. Then, use the WordPerfect Printer program to mix and match the fonts you want into a single driver.

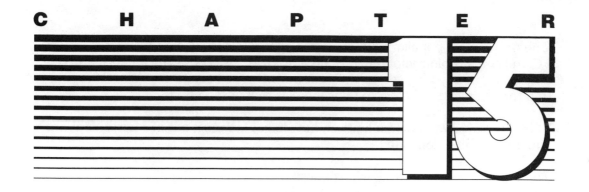

C H A P T E R

15

USING THE LASERJET +
WITH MICROSOFT WORD

One of the most popular word processing programs available today for the IBM PC and compatible computers is Microsoft Word. It is powerful and fast and can do just about anything you might want a word processor to do. Word's reputation for using laser printers to their limits is well deserved.

This chapter provides some hints on how to get the most out of Microsoft Word and a LaserJet+ compatible.

This chapter covers the following topics:

- Microsoft Word printer drivers
- Changing fonts in Microsoft Word
- Taking direct control of the printer
- Printing an envelope using Microsoft Word
- Modifying a printer driver
- Customizing your own printer driver

Microsoft includes an excellent manual on how to use printers with Word — the *Microsoft Word Printer Information Manual.* It includes not only detailed information on each printer driver and the supported features of each printer, but also detailed instructions on how to use the MAKEPRD and MERGEPRD programs to modify and customize Microsoft Word printer drivers.

The material in this chapter was developed with Microsoft Word version 4.0 and Microsoft Word MAKEPRD program version 1.50. Virtually everything in this chapter, however, also applies to versions 3.0 and 3.1 of Word and version 1.40 of MAKEPRD. The primary differences are the names of the version 3 printer drivers, which vary from the version 4 drivers. See the version 3 *Printer Information Manual.*

MICROSOFT WORD PRINTER DRIVERS

Microsoft Corporation provides dozens of printer drivers to support its software. A printer driver contains the information Microsoft Word needs to access the special features of a printer, such as the command to turn underlining on or off.

The Microsoft Word printer drivers are found in files on the Word distribution disks, which are labeled "Printers 1" and "Printers 2." These two disks contain over 100 printer drivers. Word printer drivers are in files with the file name extension .PRD.

The Word 4.0 printer driver files for LaserJet+ compatible printers are in the following files:

Drivers For Hp Cartridges: portrait

Driver File	Cartridges Supported
HPLASER1.PRD	A, B, C, D, E, G, H, J, L, Q, W, X
HPLASER2.PRD	F, K, P, R, U
HPLASER3.PRD	J, R, Z
HPLASMS.PRD	Z
HPLASRMN.PRD	F
HPLASPS.PRD	B
HPLASTAX.PRD	T
HPPCCOUR.PRD	Y

Drivers For Hp Cartridges: landscape

Driver File	Cartridges Supported
HPLASLAN.PRD	A, B, C, G, H, L, M, N, P, Q, R, U, V
HPLASMSL.PRD	Z

Figure 15.1   Word 4.0 Cartridge Printer Driver Files

Drivers For Hp Soft Fonts

Driver File	Soft Fonts Supported
HPDWNLGL.PRD	DA Landscape Fonts (Letter Gothic and Presentation)
HPDWNLGP.PRD	DA Portrait Fonts (Letter Gothic and Presentation)
HPDWNPRL.PRD	EA Landscape Fonts (Line Draw, Math fonts, Prestige)
HPDWNPRP.PRD	EA Portrait Fonts (Line Draw, Math fonts, Prestige)
HPDWNSFL.PRD	AC and AE Landscape Fonts (Helvetica and Times Roman-USASCII symbol set)
HPDWNSFP.PRD	AC and AE Portrait Fonts (Helvetica and Times Roman-USASCII symbol set)
HPDWNR8L.PRD	AD and AF Landscape Fonts (Helvetica and Times Roman-Roman 8 symbol set)
HPDWNR8P.PRD	AD and AF Portrait Fonts (Helvetica and Times Roman-Roman 8 symbol set)
HPDWNZHP.PRD	TA (Zapf Humanist)
HPDWNCNP.PRD	SA (Century Schoolbook)
HPDWNHLP.PRD	UA (Headline Fonts)
HPDWNGAP.PRD	RA (Garamond)

Figure 15.2   *Word 4.0 Soft Font Printer Driver Files*

The *Microsoft Word Printer Information* manual lists exactly what fonts and sizes each LaserJet driver supports. The number of LaserJet drivers is large because each driver supports only a few of the many fonts available on cartridges and disk. If a printer driver does not exist for the combination of fonts you are using, you can use Word's MERGEPRD program to combine elements from various drivers, or you can create your own printer driver, using the Microsoft Word MAKEPRD program.

Selecting Printer Drivers in Microsoft Word

To print a file with a particular print driver, press [ESC] [P] [O], which takes you to the Print Options menu.

```
PRINT OPTIONS printer: HPDWNR8P.PRD    setup: LPT1:
  copies: 1                            draft: Yes(No)
  hidden text: Yes(No)                 summary sheet: Yes(No)
  range: All(Selection)Pages           page numbers:
  widow/orphan control:(Yes)No         queued: Yes(No)
  feed: Manual(Continuous)Bin1 Bin2 Bin3 Mixed
Enter printer name or press F1 to select from list
```

Figure 15.3   *Print Options Menu*

The selection will be on the name of the current printer driver. To change the printer driver, simply enter the name of the driver you want. If you can't remember the names of the available drivers, simply press [F1], and Word will list the drivers for you. Use the arrow keys to move the inverse-video cursor to the driver you want, and press [Return].

Word always searches for drivers in the same subdirectory as the current driver. If you want the program to search in another subdirectory, you must specify that subdirectory when specifying the driver name in the printer field of the Print Options menu.

Adding Printer Drivers

If the list of printer drivers does not include the driver you want, simply copy them to where Word can find them. On a floppy disk system, they should be included on your Word working disk. On a hard disk, place them in your Word subdirectory if you are using only internal and cartridge fonts, or in the same subdirectory as your soft fonts.

CHANGING FONTS IN MICROSOFT WORD

To change fonts in Word, press [Alt/F8]. Word will display the Format Character menu at the bottom of the screen with the selection on the font name field.

```
FORMAT CHARACTER bold: Yes(No)      italic: Yes(No)         underline: Yes(No)
          strikethrough: Yes(No)    uppercase: Yes(No)      small caps: Yes(No)
          double underline: Yes(No) position:(Normal)Superscript Subscript
          font name: Gothic         font size: 12           hidden: Yes(No)
   Enter font name or press F1 to select from list
```

Figure 15.4   Format Character Menu

The current font selection is highlighted. Type the name of the font you want. If you are not sure, press [F1] to see what other fonts are available in the current printer driver. Move the selection with the arrow keys to the font name you want. Then, press the [Tab] key to move to the font size field. Again, type in the font size you want or, if you are not sure, press [F1] to see a listing of the font sizes available for that font with the selected printer driver. When the fields are properly set, press [Return].

The selected text will now be printed in the chosen font.

Sometimes, you may want to print in a font not supported by your printer driver. You must then change printer drivers or create a driver that contains the fonts you want to use together (discussed later in this chapter).

TAKING DIRECT CONTROL OF THE PRINTER

On rare occasions, you may need to switch to a font that is not supported by the printer driver you are using. In these cases, you will need to give the instructions directly to the printer by inserting printer controls right in your document.

You do this by using the Alternate [ALT] key and the numeric keypad. By holding down [ALT] and pressing the ASCII number of any character, you can enter that character into the document. For example, hold down [ALT] and press the numbers [2] and [7]. 27 is the ASCII number of the ESC character. A small arrow pointing to the left will appear on your screen. This is the ESC character. You can now enter the other characters in the command. Because they are almost always printable ASCII characters, you can simply enter them from the regular keyboard.

For example, if you wanted to select a page length of 65 lines, you would press [ALT/2/7] to enter ESC into your document and then enter &l65P. The command would appear on your screen as a small arrow pointing to the left, followed by &l65P. When Word sent that part of the document to the printer, the printer would reset the page length to 65 lines.

Note that Word will count the characters in your command when figuring the length of your lines, so you cannot use embedded printer commands in justified paragraphs without throwing the alignment off. If you find yourself using this technique very often (which is unlikely), you might want to create a special font in your printer driver in which every character has a width of 0.

PRINTING AN ENVELOPE USING MICROSOFT WORD

Because of Word's sophisticated formatting capabilities, printing an envelope is easy. First, clear your work space by pressing [ESC] [T] [C] [W] for Transfer Clear Window. Next, enter [ESC] [F] [D] [M] to reach the Format Division Margins menu.

```
FORMAT DIVISION MARGINS top: 2"      bottom: 1.75"   left: 1.5"   right: 1.5"
                       page length: 10.5"   width: 8"      gutter margin: 0"
              running-head position from top: 1.25"   from bottom: 1"
Enter measurement
```

Figure 15.5   Format Division Margins Menu

Set the top margin to 2.25" and the left margin to 5.5". (You might need to experiment with the left margin, depending on the paper size your printer expects when you use the manual feed slot.) Set the other two margins to 0". Set the paper size to 8" long and 14" wide. Press [Return].

Next, type your return address in the upper left corner of the screen. When you finish, space down about four lines and press [ESC] [F] [P] for the Format Paragraph menu.

```
FORMAT PARAGRAPH alignment: Left Centered Right Justified
        left indent: 0"           first line: 0"        right indent: 0"
        line spacing: 8.5 pt      space before: 0 li    space after: 0 li
        keep together: Yes(No)    keep follow: (Yes)No  side by side: Yes(No)
Select option
```

Figure 15.6   *Format Paragraph Menu*

Set the alignment to "left" and the left indent to 3.5". The rest of the format characteristics can remain the same. Press [Return].

The cursor should return to the edit screen, in the position for the address to which you are going to send the envelope. Press [Ctrl] and] (the right square bracket) at the same time. A small » should appear on the screen. Place the selection over the » and press [Alt/X] and then [E] twice, which formats the » as hidden text. The » should either disappear from the screen, be replaced by a double-headed arrow, or be underlined.

Now, save this file under the name ENVELOPE.DOC. Press [ESC] [T] [S] and, when asked for a file name, enter ENVELOPE.DOC. Store the file on the floppy disk that contains your working copy of Word or in your Word subdirectory.

Preparing a Printer Driver for Envelopes

You must prepare a printer driver to print in landscape orientation with your envelope file. The easiest way to handle this requirement is to use one of the existing Word landscape printer drivers.

Drivers For Hp Cartridges - Landscape

Driver File   Cartridges Supported

HPLASLAN.PRD   A, B, C, G, H, L, M, N, P, Q, R, U, V
HPLASMSL.PRD   Z

Drivers For Hp Soft Fonts - Landscape

Driver File   Soft Fonts Supported

HPDWNLGL.PRD   DA (Letter Gothic and Presentation)
HPDWNPRL.PRD   EA (Line Draw, Math fonts, Prestige)
HPDWNSFL.PRD   AC and AE (Helvetica and Times Roman-
                                  USASCII symbol set)
HPDWNR8L.PRD   AD and AF (Helvetica and Times Roman-
                                  Roman 8 symbol set)

Figure 15.7   Drivers for Hewlett-Packard Landscape Fonts

If none of those drivers includes the font you want, use MERGEPRD and MAKEPRD to customize your own driver (discussed later in this chapter).

Printing an Envelope

To print an envelope, load the file ENVELOPE.DOC with the Transfer Load command. Then, simultaneously press [Ctrl] and the period (.) key, which will jump the selection to the hidden ». Next, type the address.

To actually print, press [ESC] [P] [O] for the **Print Options** menu.

```
PRINT OPTIONS printer: HPLASLAN.PRD    setup: LPT1:
  copies: 1                            draft: Yes(No)
  hidden text: Yes(No)                 summary sheet: Yes(No)
  range: All(Selection)Pages           page numbers:
  widow/orphan control:(Yes)No         queued: Yes(No)
  feed: Manual Continuous Bin1 Bin2(Bin3)Mixed
Enter printer name or press F1 to select from list
```

Figure 15.8   *Print Options Menu*

Select the appropriate printer driver, such as HPLASLAN.PRD. Make sure it is a driver that supports the fonts you want in landscape mode. If you are using soft fonts, use Word's automatic font downloading capabilities to load the fonts.

Before leaving the Printer Options menu, select Bin 3 in the feed field. Bin 3 is the manual feed slot.

Now, press [Return] twice, load the envelope into the manual feed slot, and sit back and relax as your envelope prints.

MODIFYING MICROSOFT WORD PRINTER DRIVERS

The Microsoft Word MAKEPRD program gives you the ability to modify almost all the features of a Microsoft Word printer driver.

The MAKEPRD program turns a printer driver into a text file in a particular format. Details of that format are included in the *Microsoft Word Printer Information* manual that comes with Word.

You can edit the text file created by MAKEPRD with any text editor, including Microsoft Word itself. When you have finished editing, you can change the text file back into a printer driver again with MAKEPRD.

Starting MAKEPRD from a Floppy Disk System

If you are using a floppy disk system, insert your working copy of the Microsoft Word Utilities disk in drive B and the disk containing your printer drivers in drive A. Make sure you are logged on to drive A. The prompt should appear as follows:

```
A:>
```

or

```
A:\>
```

Start the MAKEPRD program by entering

```
B:MAKEPRD [Return]
```

Starting MAKEPRD from a Hard Disk System

If you are using a hard disk system, change to the directory containing the MAKEPRD program and the printer drivers. Start the program by entering

```
MAKEPRD [Return]
```

Using MAKEPRD

The MAKEPRD program will request the name of the .PRD file you want to use in addition the name of the text file.

```
W:\>MAKEPRD


PRD Editor 1.50 of July 14, 1987
Name of PRD file : HPDWNR8P.SFP
Name of Text file: HPDWNR8P.TXT
```

Usually, one of the files won't exist yet, so now is the time to make up the name. Often, you can simply change the file type to .TXT from .PRD as in the previous example.

When you have entered the names of the files, the program will ask whether you want to turn a text file into a .PRD file or turn a .PRD file into a text file.

```
Select PRD to Text conversion (Press T)
    or Text to PRD conversion (Press P):_
```

Make your choice, and the program will do the work.

Details on operating the MAKEPRD program and details on the internal format of a .PRD file are beyond the scope of this book, but you can find them in *The Power of: Microsoft Word 4.0* (also by the author, MIS:Press, 1988).

Soft Fonts

One problem that occasionally arises is that you have the "soft" disk-based version of a font for which there is only a cartridge driver. For example, you might have chosen the driver HPLASER2.PRD, which supports the Helvetica-like fonts on Hewlett-Packard's U font cartridge.

You can also, however, obtain fonts virtually identical to fonts for which there is no driver, and you can download those fonts into the printer. The only difference between the two sets of fonts is in the character sets. Cartridge fonts have the Roman-8 symbol set, while disk-based fonts use the USASCII symbol set. As a result, to select the cartridge-based fonts, you need an escape sequence that begins

ESC (8U

But to call the downloaded fonts, you will need an escape sequence that begins

ESC (0U

Because the printer driver is designed for the cartridge fonts, you will need to modify it slightly for it to work with the downloaded fonts. To perform this task, use the MAKEPRD program to convert the HPLASAX.PRD driver into a text file. Then, find the font descriptions in that text file.

Each font selection command begins with

^[(8U

The ^[stands for ESC, and the command ESC (8U selects a font with the Roman-8 symbol set.

If you change each of those commands so they begin

^[(0U

you will be asking for a font with the USASCII symbol set, which is the symbol set of the downloaded versions of the Helvetica-like fonts. (Note that you do *not* include spaces within the command string.)

This type of minor change to the font selection commands is probably the task you will most frequently perform with the Microsoft Word MAKEPRD program.

CUSTOMIZING YOUR OWN PRINTER DRIVER

Occasionally, however, you will want to make other changes to a printer driver. You may, for example, want a combination of fonts that is not available in any existing HP printer driver for Word. In such a case, use Word's MERGEPRD program to create a new driver with the fonts you want.

Sometimes, the problem can become more complex. For example, if you are using a Mannesmann Tally MT910 laser printer equipped with a cartridge-based Times Roman 10-point font, you might want to use this cartridge-based font along with several downloaded Times Roman fonts.

An obvious solution would be simply to use the HPDWNR8P.PRD printer driver, which supports 11 different sizes of Times Roman characters, including 10-point. There is a problem, however. The character widths of the cartridge-based fonts are not the same as those of the downloaded fonts. As a result, when asked to print 10-point type, Word has trouble lining up the characters at tabs and in justified paragraphs. In other words, the table containing character width information is wrong for printing with the cartridge-based font.

A little experimentation quickly reveals that the Mannesmann Tally font cartridge has the same character widths as the fonts supported by the Hewlett-Packard F cartridge. All you must do is place the character width tables from the driver for the F cartridge (HPLASRMN.PRD) into the HPDWNR8P.PRD driver you want to use.

Using MAKEPRD, you can create text files for both drivers. Then, using Word's split-screen abilities, place the text version of one driver in one window and the text version of the other driver in the other window. Finally, delete the character width tables for 10-point Times Roman from the driver HPDWNR8P.PRD and insert the width tables from HPLASRMN.PRD, remembering to renumber them.

Only rarely will you need to perform this type of manipulation on a Microsoft Word printer driver, but when you do, it is helpful that Microsoft has made their printer drivers so straightforward and accessible.

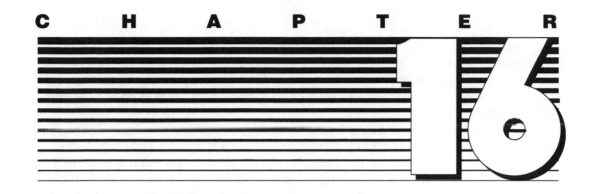

CHAPTER

16

USING THE
LASERJET + WITH PAGEMAKER

PageMaker, from Aldus Corporation, virtually created the idea of desktop publishing. When the program was first available, late in the summer of 1985, it ran only on an Apple Macintosh computer. If you wanted laser printer output, you needed Apple's expensive LaserWriter laser printer. It was easy to spend $15,000 on hardware alone.

In early 1987, PageMaker became available for the IBM PC-AT and compatibles. It also began working with the HP LaserJet+ and other printers that use the PCL printer language. As a result, desktop publishing moved to the PC world from the Macintosh world and the cost dropped by half. Today, with low-cost laser printers and AT clones available, the cost of starting out in quality desktop publishing is about a quarter of what it was in 1985.

PageMaker is philosophically different from its main competitor, Ventura Publisher. Ventura is designed for long documents with fairly simple designs, such as books. PageMaker is for shorter, layout-intensive documents, such as magazines.

PageMaker runs under Microsoft's Windows operating environment, which gives it the graphic capabilities necessary to show you what your pages will look like on the screen.

PageMaker includes built-in Helvetica and Times Roman fonts. If you want to diversify your documents with other soft fonts, you must let PageMaker know about them.

ADDING FONTS TO PAGEMAKER

Adding fonts to PageMaker involves three steps:

- First, you must create a PFM (Printer Font Metrics) file for each font. This file contains information PageMaker must know about your fonts.

- Second, you must make sure Windows and PageMaker know you are using a LaserJet+ compatible printer.

- Finally, you must edit the file WIN.INI to inform PageMaker of where to find width information about your fonts and, if necessary, where to find that information to load it into the printer.

Creating PFM Files

The program PCLPFM is in the file PCLPFM.EXE on your PageMaker Drivers disk. Copy it to the subdirectory containing your font files.

PCLPFM creates a PFM file that contains information about your font that Page-Maker must know. The PFM file has the same name as the font file, except that it converts the last letter of the file name to a P for portrait fonts or L for landscape fonts. PFM files also change the font's file name extension to .PFM. So, for example, the font file CN080BPN.SFP will have a corresponding PFM file named CN080BPP.PFM.

Running PCLPFM

When you run the PCLPFM program, it will first request the name of the font file for which you want to create a PFM file.

```
Download file name > _
( ï [Enter] to exit )
```

Enter the name of the font file. For example, to create a PFM file for the font file CN080BPN.USP, enter the file name as follows:

```
CN080BPN.USP [Return]
```

Next, the program will propose a name for the PFM file.

```
PFM (output) file name > CN080BPP.PFM
(Backspace to change)   ENTER to accept
```

Most of the time, the name will be adequate, so press [Return]. If there is already a file with that name, the program will ask if you want to overwrite that file.

The program will then read the font file and tell you what it thinks is the name of that font. This is the name that PageMaker will display in the Font Names dialog box.

```
Font name > CN*080B
(Backspace to change)   ENTER to accept
```

In the example, the font name is somewhat ambiguous. Backspace to change it to Century and then press [Return] to accept the revised name.

```
Font name > Century
(Backspace to change)   ENTER to accept
```

The next to last item, PCLPFM, asks you to designate the family of this font.

```
Family name > _
Enter R, W, M, S̄ or D for :
 Roman
 sWiss
 Modern
 Script
 Decorative
```

Roman fonts are fonts with serifs and strokes of varying widths, such as Times Roman, Century Schoolbook, and Garamond. Modern fonts, such as Optima, have no serifs and have strokes of variable widths. Swiss fonts, such as Helvetica, have strokes that are all of the same width. Script fonts imitate handwriting. Decorative fonts include fonts, such as Old English, that are used for headlines and as decoration.

Choose the correct family for this font, and press [Return].

Finally, PCLPFM will repeat your choices back to you and write the PFM file.

```
This PFM file used the Century facename.
This PFM file used the Roman family.

 CN080BPP.PFM.......696 of 696 bytes written.
```

PCLPFM then moves the cursor back to the top of the screen and requests the name of another font file for which to prepare a PFM file. Enter a new font file name, or press [Return] to exit.

Printer Information

Once you have prepared PFM files for all fonts you want to use with PageMaker, you must modify the text file WIN.INI, which tells Windows how to configure itself when it starts up.

First, you must inform WIN.INI that you are using a printer that uses Hewlett-Packard's Printer Control Language (PCL) by running CONTROL.EXE from the MS-DOS Windows Executive or by starting PageMaker and selecting the Control Panel from the System menu.

Either way, choose the Add New Printer command, which allows you to tell Windows exactly what printers are attached to your computer and to which ports they are attached.

Next, select Printer from the Setup menu and provide printer-specific information to Windows. When you click OK, Windows will add the necessary printer information to the WIN.INI file.

WIN.INI—Font Information

To inform PageMaker that you are using soft fonts, you must edit WIN.INI, using a text editor. In the section of WIN.INI that begins

```
[PageMaker]
```

you must add information about your printer and your PFM and soft font files.

Make sure there is a section of WIN.INI headed

```
[HPPCL,LPT1]
```

LPT1 might be replaced with COM1, COM2, LPT2, LPT3, or LPT4. This entry informs Windows to use a LaserJet+ compatible printer connected to a particular printer port as the printer with PageMaker.

Under the printer port entry, you need one line for each soft font you want to use.

```
SoftFontn=PFMFILE.NAM,FONTFILE.NAM
```

Each line must begin with `SoftFontn`, where `n` is a number between 1 and 32,768. For fonts that PageMaker is to load, `n` will be the LaserJet+ font ID number when this font is loaded into the printer. For "permanent" fonts loaded before you started PageMaker, `n` is the font number assigned to that font when it is loaded. These font numbers are crucial because PageMaker calls for fonts with the <u>ESC</u> (# X command and n=#.

`PFMFILE.NAM` is the name (including the path) for the PFM file for that font.

`FONTFILE.NAM` is the name (including the path) for the file that contains the font if it is to be loaded as a temporary font as needed by PageMaker. If you loaded the font earlier with font number `n` as a permanent LaserJet+ font, you do not need this part of the entry.

Following is an example of this section of a WIN.INI file, which includes information for Optima fonts. The 12-point, 14-point bold, and 24-point bold versions are loaded as permanent fonts, while the rest are to be loaded as temporary fonts when needed.

```
[HPPCL,LPT1]
Softfont1=c:\fonts\op080rpp.pfm,c:\fonts\op080rpn.usp
Softfont2=c:\fonts\op080bpp.pfm,c:\fonts\op080bpn.usp
Softfont3=c:\fonts\op080ipp.pfm,c:\fonts\op080ipn.usp
Softfont4=c:\fonts\op100rpp.pfm,c:\fonts\op100rpn.usp
Softfont5=c:\fonts\op100bpp.pfm,c:\fonts\op100bpn.usp
Softfont6=c:\fonts\op100ipp.pfm,c:\fonts\op100ipn.usp
Softfont7=c:\fonts\op120rpp.pfm
Softfont8=c:\fonts\op120bpp.pfm
Softfont9=c:\fonts\op120ipp.pfm
Softfont10=c:\fonts\op140rpp.pfm,c:\fonts\op140rpn.usp
Softfont11=c:\fonts\op140bpp.pfm
Softfont12=c:\fonts\op140ipp.pfm,c:\fonts\op140ipn.usp
Softfont13=c:\fonts\op240rpp.pfm,c:\fonts\op240rpn.usp
Softfont14=c:\fonts\op240bpp.pfm
```

Save WIN.INI, and restart PageMaker if you have PageMaker with the run-timer version of Windows, or restart Windows if you have the stand-alone version. You will find your new fonts listed on the PageMaker menus.

PAGEMAKER SCREEN FONTS

If your font manufacturer provides screen fonts, PageMaker can display fonts on the screen to resemble those that will be printed. If there are no appropriate screen fonts, PageMaker substitutes generic screen fonts; the program includes a serif, a sans serif, and a non-proportional generic screen font. Text in a generic font will not appear on screen exactly as it will on the page, but the line breaks and the overall spacing will be accurate.

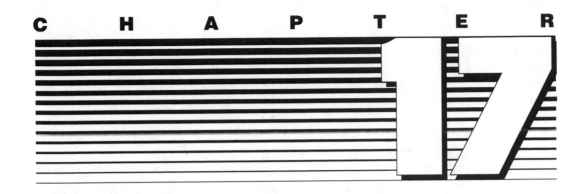

C H A P T E R

17

USING THE LASERJET +
WITH VENTURA PUBLISHER

Ventura Publisher is a powerful page-layout program that makes excellent use of the LaserJet+ and its capabilities. Ventura is a desktop publishing program of the WYSIWYG ("What you see is what you get") variety. What you see on the screen is a close approximation of what will appear on the page.

HOW TO ADD FONTS TO VENTURA

As it comes from its suppliers, Ventura works with four typefaces: Dutch (Times Roman), Swiss (Helvetica), Courier, and Symbol. As a result, documents produced on Ventura have a "desktop-published" look.

You can, however, add other fonts to Ventura. There are three steps to adding a new font in Ventura publisher:

- Copy the font to the \VENTURA subdirectory on your hard disk.

- Copy the font width table to the \VENTURA subdirectory; if there is no Ventura width table with the font, you must create a Ventura-compatible width table with the HPLTOVFM and VFMTOWID programs.

- Use Ventura's Add/Remove Font option to merge the width table for the new font with the width table for the existing font.

COPYING THE FONTS

Place your font disk in the floppy disk drive of your computer, and use the DOS COPY command to copy the font files to the VENTURA subdirectory on your hard drive. Enter the following command:

```
copy a:*.* c:\ventura [Return]
```

WIDTH TABLES

Many font suppliers now include Ventura-compatible width tables with their fonts. If the fonts you are adding include these width tables, copy them to the VENTURA subdirectory.

If the fonts do not come with Ventura-compatible width tables, you must generate them, which takes about fifteen minutes.

Creating VFM Tables

The first step is to generate Ventura Font Metric (VFM) files for your fonts with the program HPLTOVFM.EXE found on your Ventura Utilities disk (#11). VFM files contain information about the fonts and are used as part of the process of creating width tables.

The syntax for the HPLTOVFM program is as follows:

```
HPLTOVFMfontname/F={name}/N={typeface}/P={size}/W={weight}
```

`Fontname` is the name of the file containing the font; it must end with the extension .SFP if it is a portrait font or .SFL if it is a landscape font (for example, CN080RPN.SFP). You must change the names of your fonts if they don't use the SFP or SFL file extension convention. Use Dos's REName command. For example, to rename the font file HV100P.R8P to HV100P.SFP, enter

```
REN HV100P.R8p Hv100p. sfp [Return]
```

For `/F={name}`, replace `{name}` with the name you want for this font on the Ventura font menu, for example, Century, Optima, or Garamond.

For `/N={typeface}`, replace `{typeface}` with a numeric code for the font's typeface.

Typeface	N	Typeface	N
American Typewriter	100	Helvetica Narrow	50
Avant Garde	51	Helvetica-Condensed	59
Benguiat	26	Helvetica-Cond-Black	60
Bodoni	36	Helvetica-Cond-Light	58
Bodoni-Poster	37	Korinna	53
Bookman	23	Letter Gothic	105
Century Old Style	38	Lubalin	24
Century Schoolbook	20	Machine	101
Cheltenham	39	Melior	31
Courier	1	New Baskerville	33
Courier-Oblique	102	Optima	52
Franklin Gothic	56	Orator	104
Franklin Gothic Heavy	57	Palatino	2
Friz Quardrata	28	Park Avenue	35
Galliard	32	Prestige Elite	103
Garamond	22	Sonata	130
Glypha	27	Souvenir	25
Goudy	34	Symbol	128
Helvetica	2	Times	14
Helvetica Black	55	Trump Mediaeval	30
Helvetica Light	54	Zapf Chancery	29
		Zapf Dingbats	129

Figure 17.1   Ventura Typefaces and Corresponding Codes

For /P={size}, replace {size} with the font's size in points. Always use two characters, for example, 06.

For /W={weight}, replace {weight} with the code for the font's weight.

Weight	Code
Normal	N
Bold	B
Italic	I
Bold-Italic	T

Figure 17.2   *Ventura Font Weights and Corresponding Codes*

Example

Following is an example command for using the HPLTOVFM program to create a VFM file for one of Hewlett-Packard's Century Schoolbook fonts, in this case, a 12-point bold font.

```
HPLTOVFM CN120BPN.SFP /F=Century/N=20/P=12/W=B
```

Using a Batch File

Usually, you will be preparing groups of files for inclusion in Ventura. To ensure that you don't make any mistakes, use a batch file containing all of the command lines for all of the fonts for which you want to create VFM files. For example, you might use a file containing the following information to create VFM files for all the 6-, 7-, and 8-point portrait fonts in HP's Century Schoolbook font set.

```
hpltovfm CN060BPN.SFP /F=Century/N=20/P=06/W=B
hpltovfm CN060IPN.SFP /F=Century/N=20/P=06/W=I
hpltovfm CN060RPN.SFP /F=Century/N=20/P=06/W=N
hpltovfm CN070BPN.SFP /F=Century/N=20/P=07/W=B
hpltovfm CN070IPN.SFP /F=Century/N=20/P=07/W=I
hpltovfm CN070RPN.SFP /F=Century/N=20/P=07/W=N
hpltovfm CN080BPN.SFP /F=Century/N=20/P=08/W=B
hpltovfm CN080IPN.SFP /F=Century/N=20/P=08/W=I
hpltovfm CN080RPN.SFP /F=Century/N=20/P=08/W=N
```

Creating Width Tables

The next step is to turn the information in the VFM files into Ventura-compatible width tables, which requires two steps. First, prepare a file containing a list of the VFM files. Second, run the program VFMTOWID.EXE.

Using a word processor or text editor, prepare a list of the files, one file on each line, as follows:

```
CN060BPN.VFM
CN060IPN.VFM
CN060RPN.VFM
CN070BPN.VFM
CN070IPN.VFM
CN070RPN.VFM
CN080BPN.VFM
CN080IPN.VFM
CN080RPN.VFM
```

Save the file, perhaps naming it CENTURY.LST.

Second, run the VFMTOWID program, inserting the name of the file containing your list in the command line as follows:

```
VFMTOWID CENTURY.LST [Return]
```

This command will create a Ventura-compatible width table.

ADDING THE FONTS TO VENTURA

The last step in adding these fonts to Ventura is to use the Add/Remove Fonts options under Ventura's Options menu heading, which will list all the font width tables it can find and give you the chance to merge them into the current font width table.

Downloading the Fonts

Ventura Publisher automatically downloads fonts as it needs them. Now that you have informed Ventura about the fonts, it will load them into the printer as needed. Remember, the fonts must be in the Ventura subdirectory of your hard disk.

Screen Fonts

When you add fonts to Ventura, they do not automatically appear on the screen. Ventura includes generic screen fonts for fonts other than its own internal fonts. Some font manufacturers, however, also include Ventura screen fonts in their font collections. If so, you can add these screen fonts to Ventura and view a closer approximation of how your finished document will look. If screen fonts are not provided, the spacing and line breaks will probably not be correct both on screen and when printing.

Landscape Fonts

If your fonts are of portrait orientation, Ventura includes the PORTOLAN.EXE program, which creates a matching landscape font for each portrait font. The program is on disk #11—the Utilities disk. Start the PORTOLAN.EXE program, inserting in the command line the name(s) of the portrait font(s) you want to convert on the command line. The program will recognize global file name references, so the command,

```
PORTOLAN C:\VENTURA\*.SFP [Return]
```

will start the program and create landscape versions of fonts in the \VENTURA subdirectory of drive C.

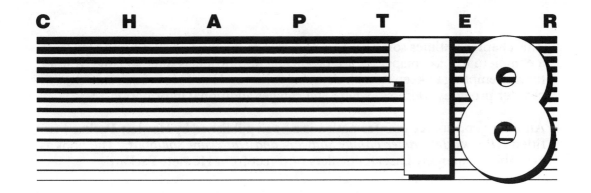

MISCELLANEOUS
LASERJET + SOFTWARE

This chapter outlines some sources of software for the LaserJet+; it is far from a complete list, as companies are producing new products almost daily. Rather than attempting to keep up with changing prices and hardware requirements, this chapter provides addresses where you can get additional information.

Another good source of information is a book published by Hewlett-Packard entitled *HP LaserJet Printer Family Software and Hardware Solutions*. The book is available from many LaserJet dealers or direct from Hewlett-Packard.

HP LaserJet Printer Family Software and Hardware Solutions
Hewlett-Packard Company
LaserJet Boise Division
1131 Chinden Blvd.
Boise, ID 83714
(800) 367-4772
(208) 323-6000

DOWNLOADABLE SOFT FONTS

When investigating font suppliers, consider a few points about their products. First, exactly what types of fonts are they offering? Fonts for the LaserJet+ fall into three categories: bit-mapped, generated, and graphic. Bit-mapped fonts are stored on disk as bit-mapped patterns that are directly downloaded to the printer.

Generated fonts do not actually exist until you ask the font generator to create them from a generalized description. The font generator then creates a bit-mapped file for downloading. For example, a font generator might have a generalized description of a Times Roman typeface. Using the font generator, you can create fonts in 8-, 10- and 12-point sizes and in regular, bold, and italic variations.

Finally, some companies that claim to offer fonts do not really offer fonts at all; instead, they offer systems that draw characters, using the raster graphics capabilities of the printer. The advantage of these systems is that they can create characters larger than the maximum font size available on the LaserJet+, but those characters take considerably longer to print; this is often a worthwhile trade-off, but you should be aware that the problem exists.

What do you intend to do with the fonts? With which programs will you use them? This information is important because, for example, fonts that work well with applications, such as Ventura Publisher, that run under the GEM operating environment are sometimes different from those that work well with Windows applications, such as PageMaker. At the same time, those fonts might not work as well as you would like with WordPerfect or Microsoft Word. So when writing for information, be sure to specify what you intend to do with the fonts and with which programs you will use them.

Third, if you will use the fonts with Ventura or PageMaker, does the company also offer screen fonts so you can get an approximation of what your page will look like when printed?

Fourth, when requesting information, ask for actual printout samples of the fonts. The quality of soft fonts varies widely from vendor to vendor.

Finally, ask font companies what other LaserJet+ products they offer. Many provide excellent font managers and font editors.

Following are some soft font programs for the LaserJet+ and compatible printers.

Conofonts

Conographic Corp.
16802 Aston, Suite 101
Irvine, CA 92714
(714) 474-1188

Conographic's fonts are good and solid. The company offers all the standard typefaces (Times Roman, Helvetica, and so on) and a few not-so-standard fonts (Old English, Dom Casual, and others). Also, they provide specialty fonts, such as fonts including elements you can use to put a border on a page. You could use these fonts to create a certificate with a fancy border or to make significant material stand out on the page.

Fontcenter Fonts

Fontcenter
580 Thousand Oaks Blvd., #198
Thousand Oaks, CA 91360
(805) 373-1919

Harvey Type

Harvey Software
PO Box 06596
Ft. Myers, FL 33906
(813) 482-8600
(800) 231-0296

HP Soft Fonts

Hewlett-Packard Company
LaserJet — Boise Division
1131 Chinden Blvd.
Boise, ID 83714
(800) 367-4772
(208) 323-6000

Hewlett-Packard markets fonts from Bitstream, a company widely reputed to produce the best laser fonts. The selection is not particularly extensive (15 typefaces in various sizes), but unless you want your documents to look like lessons in typography, these fonts are more than you will probably ever need to use.

Proofwriter Turbofonts

Image Processing Systems
6409 Appalachian Way
PO Box 5016
Madison, WI 53705
(608) 233-6093
(608) 233-5033

Fontpac Font Generator

Metro Software
2509 North Campbell Avenue
Suite 214
Tucson, AZ 85719
(602) 299-7313

Metro's Fontpac offers fifteen typefaces. Fortunately, they are not the standard typefaces available from every company. The company does offer a typeface similar to Times Roman (named "Times") and a Helvetica clone (named "New Swiss"), but they also offer some interesting different faces. When you use Fontpac with Metro's Printility printer utility program (discussed later in this chapter), Fontpac can handle fonts from 4 to 48 points high.

Downloadable Fonts

Prosoft
7248 Bellaire Ave.
North Hollywood, CA 91605
(818) 765-4444

Laserfonts/Fontware Font Generator

Softcraft
16 N. Carroll Street
Suite 500
Madison, WI 53703
(608) 257-3300
(800) 351-0500

Specific Fonts

Specific Solutions
1898 Anthony Court
Mountain View, CA 94040
(415) 941-3941

Specific Solutions points out that their fonts are primarily for use with programs running under the GEM operating environment, such as Ventura Publisher.

Zfonts

Straightforward
15000 Halldale, #115
Gardena, CA 90247
(818) 762-8150

Glyphix Font Generator

SWFTE International Ltd.
Box 5773
Wilmington, DE 19808
(302) 733-0956

Glyphix was one of the earlier font generator systems. The company received favorable reviews and now offers more than two dozen different typefaces.

Floppy Fonts

The Font Factory
PO Box 5429
Kingwood, TX 77339
(713) 358-6954

Qume Office Series Typefaces

Qume Corporation
500 Yosemite Dr.
Milpitas, CA   95035
(408) 942 4000
(800) 543-6687

Vinh Fonts

Vinh Company
214 Manfred St.
Alhambra, CA 91801
(818) 576-0488

VS Library of Fonts

VS Software
PO Box 6158
Little Rock, AK 72216
(501) 376-2083

LJ Fonts

Weaver Graphics
Fox Pavilion
Box 1132
Jenkintown, PA 19046
(215) 884-9286

FONT EDITORS AND FONT MANAGERS

A font editor is a program that allows you to display soft font characters on the screen. You can change them as needed. For example, if you have a font that contains the tilde character (~), but you really need a diamond (◇), a font editor allows you to create the new character on the screen and add it to the font in place of the old character.

Font managers generally allow you to automatically download fonts and may also create printer drivers for popular programs or create fonts from scanned images (for example, a font that contains your signature so you can automatically print it on letters).

A font editor often includes a font manager, which is why they are discussed together in this section.

Not all listed programs perform all these tasks, and many of them perform other tasks as well. Again, the best advice is to call or write for information on the latest version of the product.

In particular, make sure that the program can be command-line-driven, which means that it can download the fonts you use day after day from a batch file. If you need to start a program and load files one at a time from a menu every day, you will quickly tire of that program.

Many fonts come with font editor/managers; ask about them when you request information.

Following are some font editor and manager programs.

Conofont Manager

Conographic Corp.
16802 Aston, Suite 101
Irvine, CA 92714
(714) 474-1188

The Conofont Manager does a good job of creating WordPerfect and Microsoft Word printer drivers for a group of fonts. It also will quickly download a related group of fonts, even though you must open the program and press a few keys to do so.

Hot Lead

Harvey Software
PO Box 06596
Ft. Myers, FL 33906
(617) 354-1999
(813) 482-8600

HP PCLPak

Hewlett-Packard Company
LaserJet — Boise Division
1131 Chinden Blvd.
Boise, ID 83714
(800) 367-4772
(208) 323-6000

Despite being a Hewlett-Packard product, PCLPak is a bit of a disappointment. While it allows you to download fonts, it is menu-driven and not command-line-driven, which makes it difficult to use often.

Poems Font Editing System

Poems
509 Marin Street, #121
Thousand Oaks, CA 91360
(805) 373-1919

Personalfont

Straightforward
15000 Halldale, #115
Gardena, CA 90247
(818) 762-8150

Microsoft Word Font Manager/WordPerfect Font Managers

SWFTE International Ltd.
Box 5773
Wilmington, DE 19808
(302) 733-0956

FontGen IV/VS Tools

VS Software
PO Box 6158
Little Rock, AK 72216
(501) 376-2083

PRINTER UTILITIES

Printer utilities are programs that help you control a LaserJet+ or compatible printer. Often, they are memory-resident, meaning the computer loads them once, and they remain in memory. Usually, they intercept data on the way to the printer and either pass it through unchanged, if it is just text, or convert it to appropriate LaserJet+ commands, if it is special data designed to get the printer to perform a particular task. Also, printer utilities often allow you to integrate graphics in text, even in programs that don't normally allow you to combine text and pictures.

Following are some printer utility programs.

Inset

American Programmers Guild, Ltd.
12 Mill Plain Road
Danbury, CT 06811

Inset is simple in its aims; it describes itself as "the graphics and text integrator." Its job is to allow you to imbed graphic images in your text. It allows you to resize, rotate, and manipulate the images in other ways before inserting them into your document.

Printility

Metro Software
2509 North Campbell Avenue
Suite 214
Tucson, AZ 85719
(602) 299-7313

Printility offers font changes through embedded print commands; it can merge graphics for virtually any source and almost any resolution. The utility also includes a font manager to automatically download fonts to the printer when necessary. It is memory-resident and can pop up to present you with options as needed.

Polaris Print Merge

Polaris Software
613 West Valley Parkway
Suite 323
Escondido, CA 92925
(619) 743-7800

Print Merge also allows you to change fonts, print block and pattern graphics, and integrate graphics into your documents. It is a memory-resident program.

LASERJET+ EMULATORS

A LaserJet+ emulator is a program that will make a laser printer that is not compatible with the LaserJet+ become compatible.

LaserTwin

Metro Software
2509 North Campbell Avenue
Suite 214
Tucson, AZ 85719
(602) 299-7313

LaserTwin makes a Canon LBP-8 printer operate like a LaserJet+, which is something of a feat because, as one Metro Software engineer termed it, "The Canon printer is 100% incompatible with the LaserJet+." (Canon manufactures the printer engines used by Hewlett-Packard and has agreed that they will not directly compete with Hewlett-Packard.) LaserTwin also works with Canon printers that are relabelled and sold under other brand names such as NCR and Data General. According to the Metro Software, the program works for all HP traits, including undocumented features and error-handling characteristics.

GRAPHICS EDITORS

A graphics editor is a program that lets you manipulate LaserJet+ graphics images in the computer and then load them into the machine. For example, you may have a set of "stock art" for the LaserJet+. Using a graphics editor, you can select one image from a "sheet" of many, enlarge it, rotate it, crop it, and load it into the printer as a macro or a special font character. If you want to do much in the way of fancy graphics manipulation, or if you just want to have your laser printer insert your signature at the bottom of your letters, then you need a graphics editor.

SLED

VS Software
Box 6158
Little Rock, AR 72216
(501) 376-2083

VS Software calls SLED a "Graphics Power Tool for the laser printer." It can save a laser image as a character in a font so your signature can simply be the only letter in this font. When you need to sign your letters, just enter that character, switch to the appropriate font, and let the printer do the work.

FORM GENERATORS

Form generators are programs you can use to create fill-in-the-blank forms such as job application forms, message pads, and invoices. If you regularly create a number of these forms, a form-generating program can save you a lot of money in typesetting and printing costs.

Following are some form generator programs.

FormWorx

Analytx International, Inc.
1365 Massachusetts Avenue
Arlington, MA 02174
(617) 641-0400

FormTool

BLOC Development Corporation
1301 Dade Blvd.
Miami Beach, FL 33139
(305) 531-5486

Microsoft Word 4.0

Microsoft Corporation
16011 NE 36th Way
Box 97017
Redmond, WA 98073-9717
(206) 882-8080

You probably don't think of Microsoft Word as a form-generation program, but with the line-drawing features added in Word version 4.0, you can use Word for drawing most forms without the expense of a separate form-generation program. For more information on using Word as a form generator, see *The Power of: Microsoft Word 4.0* (also by the author, MIS:Press, 1988).

SCREEN CAPTURE PROGRAMS

Screen capture programs help you print what is on your screen, but with much more sophistication than comes with simply using the PrtSc key. These programs allow you to print graphic screens as well as text screens. These programs are memory-resident; they can pop up whenever you need them.

HotShot

SymSoft
P.O. Box 4477
Mountain View, CA 94040
(415) 941-1552

Hotshot is an excellent screen-capture utility. It works in almost any situation, including with Windows and other sophisticated graphics screens. It not only lets you capture screens, it lets you modify their contents before saving them to disk for later printing.

HP Print Screen Utility

Hewlett-Packard Company
LaserJet — Boise Division
1131 Chinden Blvd.
Boise, ID 83714
(800) 367-4772
(208) 323-6000

Hewlett-Packard's Print Screen Utility works, and it costs nothing because it resides in the printer. It is a nifty little program that will dump the contents of your screen, whatever they may be, to a LaserJet+ (or Hewlett-Packard Thinkjet). You can easily control the orientation of the image, where you want the screen image on your page, and whether or not you want the printer to eject the paper at the end of the print job. The standard command for using this utility is [Shift/PrtSc]. For further information, consult Hewlett-Packard documentation for this utility.

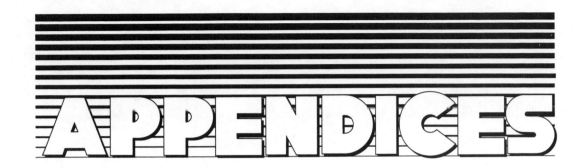

APPENDICES

APPENDIX A: COMPUTER MATHEMATICS

Computers "know" only two things: 1 and 0. Inside the computer, these numbers are represented by two electrical voltages, HIGH (1) and LOW (0). Computers compensate for their lack of knowledge with speed. They can interpret ones or zeros millions of times a second and seem to be doing more complicated things.

Because your computer and the processor in the LaserJet+ compatible printer actually only understand 1 and 0, the conventional method of counting using ten digits — from 0 to 9 — really doesn't mean much to them. Several other number systems, however, are much closer to the way the computer works, so the computer and computer users can use and understand those systems much more easily.

Due to the proliferation of number systems, when you read most computer manuals, you may find the number 10 written as $0A_H$ (in hexadecimal) or 00001010 (in binary).

Many software producers require that you use hexadecimal, ASCII, or even binary numbers to efficiently customize their programs. In particular, if you want to use all the special features of a LaserJet+ compatible printer, you may need to do a little "patching" when you use these systems for everything to run as well as possible.

DECIMAL OR BASE TEN

As you probably already know, the decimal numbering system uses the position of a digit to signify its value: the "ones" place, the "tens" place, the "hundreds" place, the "thousands" place, and so on.

If you look at the relationship between the various positions, you will notice that it is exponential, which means that each position in a number is related to the positions on either side of it through a change in the exponent or power to which the base of the number system — in this case, ten — is raised.

The first position (the one farthest to the right in a number) is referred to as the "ones" place. One is 10 raised to the power of 0, or 10^0. Any value raised to the zero power is 1; even $0^0 = 1$.

The next position to the left is referred to as the "tens" place, and $10^1 = 10$.

The next position to the left is the "hundreds" column, and $10^2 = 100$.

Notice the pattern, which can be extended indefinitely:

10^5	10^4	10^3	10^2	10^1	10^0
100,000	10,000	1,000	100	10	1

Again, because each column is related to the next one by a change in the exponent, the relationship is referred to as "exponential."

Symbols

It is important to remember that numbers are really just symbols for ideas. The symbol "1" signifies a single thing, but another symbol such as ? or ∇ could have been used to signify that amount. The particular symbol used to represent a quantity is not important, just the quantity itself.

HEXADECIMAL OR BASE SIXTEEN

Computer scientists use a "base sixteen" number system and refer to it as a "hexadecimal" number system. The system borrows the first six letters of the alphabet and uses them as numbers. (Remember, numbers are just symbols.) To make sure that everyone knows a letter is being used as a number, the letter is always preceded by a recognizable number. You will often see hexadecimal numbers such as "0A" or "2AB3"; you also will see hexadecimal numbers followed by an H (sometimes subscript) as in $0A_H$.

Exponential Relationship

The key to understanding hexadecimal numbers is to remember the exponential relationship of the base ten system. The "places" in hexadecimal numbers are related by the exponents, but, because the base is sixteen, the results are different:

16^4	16^5	16^4	16^1	16^0
65,536	4,096	256	16	1

If you already know a little about computers, some of those numbers may look familiar. 256 is the number of "characters" in a computer's alphabet, and 65,536 = 64K, or the number of memory locations used in many older computers.

Counting on Sixteen Fingers

The hexadecimal counting system is as follows:

Hex:	1	2	3	4	5	6	7	8	9
Decimal:	1	2	3	4	5	6	7	8	9

Hex:	0A	0B	0C	0D	0E	0F	10	11	12
Decimal:	10	11	12	13	14	15	16	17	18

Note that after the value normally referred to as "ten," the sequence continues with 0A and 0B. (The leading zeros keep users from mistaking the symbols "A" and "B" for letters. In this case, A and B are numbers—the same as "3" and "7.") See Appendix C for a more extensive comparison.

BINARY OR BASE TWO

If the computer "knows" only 1 and 0, it must be working with yet another number system. If the base ten system has ten digits, and the base sixteen system has sixteen digits, then a system of counting with only two digits, 1 and 0, must be a base two, or a "binary," system.

The exponential relationship for a binary system is as follows:

2^7	2^6	2^5	2^4	2^3	2^2	2^1	2^0
128	64	32	16	8	4	2	1

The binary number 101 would be equal to 5 in the base ten system because the first 1 is in the 4s column, there is a 0 in the 2s column, and there is a 1 in the 1s column: $4 + 0 + 1 = 5$. 111 in binary would be equal to 7 in the base ten system (1 "four" + 1 "two" + 1 "one" = 7).

WHY NOT JUST USE BASE 10?

Note that 16, the base of the hexadecimal number system, is in the list of "places" for the binary system, but 10 is nowhere to be seen. It is much easier and faster for a binary-based computer to work with numbers such as 16, 8, 128, 256, and 65,536 than it is for it to work with numbers based on 10.

APPENDIX B: ASCII

A **bit** is a HIGH or LOW voltage inside a computer that represents a 1 or a 0. A group of bits is referred to as a **byte.**

Most often, bytes are 8, 16, or — in newer and more powerful computers — 32 and even 64 bits long. Each byte is one character, such as a letter, a punctuation mark, or a number. A byte can also be used to instruct the computer's CPU (central processing unit) what to do.

In older microcomputers, data moved through the system in 8-bit bytes, usually moving simultaneously down eight parallel wires. Today, data usually moves in groups of 16 or 32 bits, but data is often still transferred between computers and most peripherals, such as printers, in 8-bit bytes.

Think of 8-bit bytes as 8-digit binary numbers (see Appendix A); they are a collection of eight HIGHs and LOWs inside the computer, but they can be represented as a collection of eight ones and zeros.

ASCII

Remember, the bytes are just numbers, or quantities, and you can use any symbols you want to represent those quantities.

In the computing world, some of those symbols have been standardized. The first 128 of the possible 256 available 8-bit bytes have been standardized in a system called ASCII, an acronym for American Standard Code for Information Interchange. Each of the first 128 numbers has been assigned a character. There were enough numbers so that a number could be assigned to each of the uppercase and lowercase letters, numbers, punctuation marks, and special characters referred to as control characters.

If you send the byte designated in ASCII for the letter "a" to any computer, it will display it on the screen as an "a," store it in a file as an "a," and so on. (That byte, by the way, is eight bits in the binary pattern 01100001. That binary number is equivalent to 97 decimal or 61 hexadecimal.)

More importantly for purposes discussed in this text, when you send that particular collection of bits to your printer, the computer inside the printer also knows to interpret those bits as an "a" and prints them on the page as an "a."

Examine the chart in Appendix C, which lists the ASCII code in numeric sequence with the decimal and hexadecimal numbers for each character and the characters themselves that represent those numbers.

CONTROL CODES

The first 32 ASCII codes—numbers 0 through 31—are referred to as control characters. These characters do not print or appear on the screen; instead, they control the function of a computer terminal or printer by performing tasks such as advancing the print position to the next line (line feed) or advancing the print position to the next horizontal tab stop (horizontal tab). Control codes were originally used to control early computers, and many of their functions are obsolete, but their names remain. As a result, some control codes have names such as "shift in" or "unit separator."

You may also hear control codes referred to as "Control-A" or "Control-B." Often, the word "control" is replaced by the caret character (e.g., ^A).

THE ESCAPE CODE

Pay special attention to the control code named Escape (ESC). While it is technically just another control character, it has a special status because it is used almost exclusively to signify that the following character should not to be printed but should be interpreted as a command.

For example, if your computer sends the character E to a LaserJet+ compatible printer, the printer will print the letter E on the page. If you send ESC and then E, however, your printer won't print anything but will respond to the E as a command to reset the printer back to its status when it was first turned on.

Whenever ESC precedes another control code or normally printable character, the printer will interpret the ESC sequence as a command and not as a character to be printed.

APPENDIX C: ASCII TABLE

Dec.	Hex.	ASCII	Abbr.
00	00	^@	NUL
01	01	^A	SOII
02	02	^B	STX
03	03	^C	ETX
04	04	^D	EOT
05	05	^E	ENQ
06	06	^F	ACK
07	07	^G	BEL
08	08	'H	BS
09	09	^I	HT
10	0A	^J	LF
11	0B	^K	VT
12	0C	^L	FF
13	0D	^M	CR
14	0E	^N	SO
15	0F	^O	SI
16	10	^P	DLE
17	11	^Q	DC1
18	12	^R	DC2
19	13	^S	DC3
20	14	^T	DC4
21	15	^U	NAK
22	16	^V	SYN
23	17	^W	ETB
24	18	^X	CAN
25	19	^Y	EM
26	1A	^Z	SUB
27	1B	^[	ESC

Dec.	Hex.	ASCII	
28	1C	^\	FS
29	1D	^]	GS
30	1E	^^	RS
31	1F	^–	US
32	20		SPACE
33	21	!	
34	22	"	
35	23	#	
36	24	$	
37	25	%	
38	26	&	
39	27	'	
40	28	(	
41	29	)	
42	2A	*	
43	2B	+	
44	2C	,	
45	2D	–	
46	2E	.	
47	2F	/	
48	30	0	
49	31	1	
50	32	2	
51	33	3	
52	34	4	
53	35	5	
54	36	6	
55	37	7	

continued...

Dec.	Hex.	ASCII		Dec.	Hex.	ASCII
56	38	8		92	5C	\
57	39	9		93	5D	]
58	3A	:		94	5E	^
59	3B	;		95	5F	_
60	3C	<		96	60	`
61	3D	=		97	61	a
62	3E	>		98	62	b
63	3F	?		99	63	c
64	40	@		100	64	d
65	41	a		101	65	e
66	42	b		102	66	f
67	43	c		103	67	g
68	44	d		104	68	h
69	45	e		105	69	i
70	46	f		106	6A	j
71	47	g		107	6B	k
72	48	h		108	6C	l
73	49	i		109	6D	m
74	4A	j		110	6E	n
75	4B	k		111	6F	o
76	4C	l		112	70	p
77	4D	m		113	71	q
78	4E	n		114	72	r
79	4F	o		115	73	s
80	50	p		116	74	t
81	51	q		117	75	u
82	52	r		118	76	v
83	53	s		119	77	w
84	54	t		120	78	x
85	55	u		121	79	y
86	56	v		122	7A	z
87	57	w		123	7B	{
88	58	x		124	7C	|
89	59	y		125	7D	}
90	5A	z		126	7E	~
91	5B	[		127	7	DEL

Abbreviations

NUL	Null
SOH	Start of Head
SOT	Start of Text
ETX	End of Text
EOT	End of Transmission
ENQ	Enquiry
ACK	Acknowledge
BEL	Bell (Beeper)
BS	Backspace
HT	Horizontal Tab
LF	Line Feed
VT	Vertical Tab
FF	Form Feed
CR	Carriage Return
SO	Shift Out
SI	Shift In
DLE	Data Link Escape
DC1	Device Control 1 (XON)
DC2	Device Control 2
DC3	Device Control 3 (XOFF)
DC4	Device Control 4
NAK	Negative Ack.
SYN	Synchronous Idle
ETB	End Trans. Block
CAN	Cancel
EM	End of Medium
SUB	Substitute
ESC	Escape
FS	File Separator
GS	Group Separator
RS	Record Separator
US	Unit Separator
DEL	Delete

APPENDIX D: SYMBOL SETS

ROMAN-8, USASCII, AND ROMAN EXTENDED

The Roman-8 character set is really a combination of the USASCII and Roman Extended sets. In Roman-8, the international symbols have ASCII values 128 higher than in the Roman Extended set. For example, in the Roman Extended set, the ASCII value for £ is 57. In the Roman-8 character set it is 185 (57 + 128).

!"#$%&()*+,-./0123456789:;< = >?@
ABCDEFGHIJKLMNOPQRSTUVWXYZ[\]^_`
abcdefghijklmnopqrstuvwxyz{|}~

USASCII

ÀÂÈÊËÎÏ´`^¨¯ÙÛ£¯ °ÇçÑñ¡¿¤£¥§ƒ¢ê
ôûáéóúàèòùäëöüÅîØÆåíøæÄìÖÜÉïßÔÁÃã
ÐðÍÌÓÒÕõŠšÚŸÿÞþ   —¼½ªº«■»±

Roman Extended

!"#$%&()*+,-./0123456789:;< = >?@
ABCDEFGHIJKLMNOPQRSTUVWXYZ[\]^_`
abcdefghijklmnopqrstuvwxyz{|}~
ÀÂÈÊËÎÏ´`^¨¯ÙÛ£¯ °ÇçÑñ¡¿¤£¥§ƒ¢ê
ôûáéóúàèòùäëöüÅîØÆåíøæÄìÖÜÉïßÔÁÃã
ÐðÍÌÓÒÕõŠšÚŸÿÞþ   —¼½ªº«■»±

Roman-8

MAJOR FOREIGN SYMBOL SETS

The following chart shows the character substitutions in the major foreign language symbol sets used on the LaserJet+:

ASCII #	35	36	64	91	92	93	94	96	123	124	125	126
US (8U, 0U)	#	$	@	[	\	]	^	`	{	|	}	~
UK (1E)	£	$	@	[	\	]	^	`	{	|	}	~
German (0G)	£	$	§	Ä	Ö	Ü	^	`	ä	ö	ü	ß
French (0F)	£	$	à	●	ç	§	^	`	é	ù	è	..
Swed/Finn (0S)	#	¤	É	Ä	Ö	Å	Ü	é	ä	ö	å	ü
Dan/Nor (0D)	#	$	@	Æ	Ø	Å	^	`	æ	ø	å	~
Spanish (1S)	#	$	@	¡	Ñ	¿	●	`	{	ñ	}	~
Italian (0I)	#	$	§	●	ç	é	^	ù	à	ò	è	ì
Japanese (1J)	#	$	@	[	¥	]	^	`	{	|	}	~
English 2 (2E)	#	£	@	[	\	]	^	`	{	|	}	~

APPENDIX E: SAMPLE PROGRAM

This section contains an additional program that demonstrates the capabilities of a LaserJet+ compatible printer. Like the other programs in this book, this program is written in Microsoft QuickBASIC version 4.0.

COMPATIBILITY

The program included in this Appendix was debugged using a Mannesmann Tally MT910 as reference. This program may not work in exactly the same way with your laser printer; few laser printers are 100% compatible with the LaserJet+ or with each other, despite their manufacturer's claims. Usually, these differences don't create any serious problems, but sometimes they can. For example, a LaserJet Series II printer acts on a reset command after it has processed all the commands it received before the reset. The MT910 acts on a reset command immediately. These types of minor differences can be quite irritating, and the only way you'll find them is through unhappy experience.

Assume nothing about compatibility. Never assume that all printers use the same default fonts, line spacing, or any other parameter; explicitly set parameters as you want them.

ASSIGN FONT NUMBERS

This program assigns font numbers to the three resident HP-style fonts found in an MT910 (Courier HP, Prestige HP, and Gothic HP) as well as to six fonts contained on the Mannesmann Tally Dutch 801 and Letter Gothic font cartridges. Finally, the program prints samples of each font with its corresponding font number.

```
' ASSIGN FONT NUMBERS TO THREE RESIDENT
' AND SIX CARTRIDGE FONTS IN MT910

e$=chr$(27)        ' ESCape = e$

' ======= FONT 1 - COURIER HP =======

lprint e$;"(8U";e$;"(s0p10h12v0s0b3T";   ' call Courier HP
lprint chr$(15);                          ' call primary font
lprint e$;"*c1D";                         ' assign font ID
lprint e$;"*c6F";                         ' make temporary

' ======= FONT 2 - PRESTIGE HP =======

lprint e$;"(8U";e$;"(s0p12h12v0s0b3T";   ' call Prestige HP
lprint chr$(15);                          ' call primary font
lprint e$;"*c2D";                         ' assign font ID
lprint e$;"*c6F";                         ' make temporary

' ======= FONT 3 - LINE PRINTER HP =======

lprint e$;"(8U";e$;"(s0p16.66h12v0s0b6T";    ' call Line Print
lprint chr$(15);                              ' call primary font
lprint e$;"*c3D";                             ' assign font ID
lprint e$;"*c6F";                             ' make temporary


' ======= FONT 4 - GOTHIC 12 MEDIUM =======

lprint e$;"(8U";e$;"(s0p12h12v0s0b6T";   ' call Gothic 12
                                          ' Med.
lprint chr$(15);                          ' call primary font
lprint e$;"*c4D";                         ' assign font ID
lprint e$;"*c6F";                         ' make temporary

' ======= FONT 5 - GOTHIC 12 ITALIC =======

lprint e$;"(8U";e$;"(s0p12h12v1s0b6T";   ' call Gothic 12
                                          ' Italic
lprint chr$(15);                          ' call primary font
lprint e$;"*c5D";                         ' assign font ID
lprint e$;"*c6F";                         ' make temporary
```

continued...

...from previous page

```
' ======= FONT 6 - GOTHIC 12 BOLD =======

lprint e$;"(8U";e$;"(s0p12h12v0s3b6T";   ' call Gothic
                                         ' 12 Bold
lprint chr$(15);                         ' call primary font
lprint e$;"*c6D";                        ' assign font ID
lprint e$;"*c6F";                        ' make temporary

' ======= FONT 7 - DUTCH 10 MEDIUM =======

lprint e$;"(8U";e$;"(s1p10v0s0b5T";      ' call Dutch
                                         '10 Med.
lprint chr$(15);                         ' call primary font
lprint e$;"*c7D";                        ' assign font ID
lprint e$;"*c6F";                        ' make temporary

' ======= FONT 8 - DUTCH 10 ITALIC =======

lprint e$;"(8U";e$;"(s1p10v1s0b5T";      ' call Dutch
                                         ' 10 Italic
lprint chr$(15);                         ' call primary font
lprint e$;"*c8D";                        ' assign font ID
lprint e$;"*c6F";                        ' make temporary

' ======= FONT 9 - DUTCH 10 BOLD =======

lprint e$;"(8U";e$;"(s1p10v0s3b5T";      ' call Dutch
                                         ' 10 Bold
lprint chr$(15);                         ' call primary font
lprint e$;"*c9D";                        ' assign font ID
lprint e$;"*c6F";                        ' make temporary
```

continued...

...from previous page

```
lprint e$;"(1XFont 1 - Courier HP"
lprint e$;"(2XFont 2 - Prestige HP"
lprint e$;"(3XFont 3 - Gothic HP"
lprint e$;"(4XFont 4 - Gothic 12 Medium"
lprint e$;"(5XFont 5 - Gothic 12 Italic"
lprint e$;"(6XFont 6 - Gothic 12 Bold"
lprint e$;"(7XFont 7 - Dutch 10 Medium"
lprint e$;"(8XFont 8 - Dutch 10 Italic"
lprint e$;"(9XFont 9 - Dutch 10 Bold"

lprint e$;"(1X"                        ' reset default to
                                       ' Courier HP

lprint chr$(12)                        ' Form Feed to
                                       ' print page

end
```

INDEX

D

Descriptor, 61-69
Display functions, 161
DOS, 3
Dots, 89, 93
Downloaded fonts, *See* Fonts, soft
Dutch, 48, 69

E

EAN/UPC symbol set, 37
Elite, 48, 69
End of line wrap, 105, 109
    default, 157
English symbol set, 37
Envelope printing, 160
    Microsoft Word, 209
    WordPerfect, 192
Environment, 146
Epson, 25, 166
ESC, 8, 12, 256
ESC (s # W, 70
ESC #l # L, 116
ESC &a # L, 110, 116
ESC &a # M, 110, 116
ESC &a # R, 97-98, 112
ESC &d @, 156
ESC &d D, 156
ESC &f # S, 88, 93
ESC &f # X, 145-148
ESC &f # Y, 144, 148
ESC &k # G, 97, 105
ESC &k # H, 103, 104
ESC &k # S, 41
ESC &l # 0, 33
ESC &l # C, 96, 99, 126
ESC &l # D, 96, 100, 115
ESC &l # E, 111, 115
ESC &l # F, 114-115
ESC &l # H, 98, 159
ESC &l # L, 114
ESC &l # P, 113, 115

Inset, 242
IRV symbol set, 37
ISO symbol set, 37
Italian symbol set, 37
Italic, 23, 44, 67

J

Japanese symbol set, 37

K

Kana-8 symbol set, 37
Korinna, 48, 69
Kyocera, 166

L

Landscape orientation, 19, 33
Languages
  EXPRESS, 170
  Printer Control Language (PCL), 13, 166
  QuickBASIC, 3
Laserfont/Fontware Font Generator, 237
LaserJet software emulators, 243
LaserTwin, 244
LaserWriter, 3, 166
Latin ISO symbol set, 37
Leading, 23
Letter Gothic, 48, 69
LE, 96, 109
  action, 105
Line
  height, 23
  spacing, 23
Line draw symbol set, 37
Line feed, 96, 109
  action, 105
  half, 97

Q

R

Reverse half-line feed, 98
Reverse line feed, 97
Ricoh, 166
ROM, 18
Roman extended symbol set, 21, 37
Roman-8 symbol set, 21, 37
Rows, 91

S

Screen capture software, 246
  Screen fonts
  PageMaker, 223
Ventura Publisher, 231
Script, 48, 69
Secondary font, 28
Self-test, 158
Shift In, 28, 50
Shift Out, 28
SI, 28, 50, 103
Side margins, *See* Margins, side
SLED graphics editor, 244
SO, 28, 103
Soft fonts, *See* Fonts, soft
Souvenir, 48, 69
SPACE, 9, 22
Spacing, 22, 38, 64
Spanish HP symbol set, 37
Spanish ISO/IBM symbol set, 37
Specific Fonts, 237
Starting position
  fixing, 157
Stroke weight, 45, 68
Swedish symbol set, 37
Swedish/Finnish symbol set, 37
Swiss, 48, 69
Symbol sets, 21, 24-25, 36, 65
  7-bit, 37
  8-bit, 37
  codes, 37
  Roman extended, 21, 261

Roman-8, 21, 261
substitution table, 262
table, 37
USASCII , 21, 261

T

Tab, 106
Temporary font, 51-55, 58, 76
Times Roman, 24, 47-48, 69
TMS RMN, 48, 69
Top margin, *See* Margins, top
Toshiba, 166
Transparent print data, 161
Trays
  paper, 159
Typeface, 24, 47, 68-69
  table, 48

U

Underline, 156
Universal Product Code (UPC), 37
University Roman, 48, 69
Upright characters, 44
Upright fonts, 23
US legal symbol set, 37
Utilities, 242

V

Ventura Publisher
  fonts, 226
    adding, 230
  HPLTOVFM program, 227
  screen fonts, 231
  Ventura Font Metric files, 227
    width tables, 230
Vertical motion index, 96, 99, 111, 157

Vinh Fonts, 239
VMI, *See* Vertical Motion Index
VS Library of Fonts, 239
VS Tools, 242

W

Width tables, 173
Windows, 37
Word, Microsoft, *See* Microsoft Word
WordPerfect
  direct printer command, 191
  embedded printer commands, 191
  font selection, 188
  manual feed, 186
  paper cassettes, 186
  printer drivers, 178
    adding, 184
    custom, 200
    modifying, 195
    selecting, 181
    printer help program, 179-180
    sheet feeders, 186
    soft fonts, 202
  WordPerfect Font Manager, 241

X

Xerox, 166

Z

Zapf Calligraphic, 48, 69
Zapf Humanist, 48, 69
ZFonts, 238

RELATED TITLES FROM MIS:PRESS

WordPerfect 5.0
A comprehensive guide to WordPerfect, covering all the new desktop publishing features of version 5.0, including bit stream fonts, stylesheets, various typefaces, and integrating graphics with text. This book addresses both new users and those already familiar with WordPerfect who are looking for upgrade information.

Rob Krumm   0-943518-97-0 $19.95

Microsoft Word 4.0
This book is a comprehensive guide to learning and using Microsoft Word 4.0. Describes how Word 4.0 interacts with desktop publishing system; outlines commands and procedures for developing and using style sheets; and offers examples and illustrations.

Timothy Perrin   0-943518-31-8 $19.95

Running PC-DOS 3.3
An essential desktop reference guide for all PC users. Easier to use and understand than the DOS manual, this book's clear organization, concise instructions, and illustrations help users make the most of their computer's operating system. Includes version 3.3

Carl Siechert and Chris Wood   0-943518-47-4 $22.95

Ventura
An easy-to-understand guide·focusing exclusively on Ventura 1.1, the best-selling desktop publishing software program for the IBM PC. Emphasizes the basics of using Ventura as well as how to design documents such as reports, invoices, newsletters, and multi-chapter publications.

Rob Krumm   0-943518-37-7 $21.95

Advanced DOS
An indispensable resource and reference guide for serious DOS programmers. Includes sections on data storage, BIOS and DOS interrupts, utility programming, and memory-resident utilities.

Michael I. Hyman   0-943518-83-0 $22.95
$44.95 w/disk

Microsoft Windows Program Development
Outlining specific procedures and techniques for programming in Microsoft Windows, this book covers memory management, device independence communications interface, standard graphics interface, software and hardware compatibility, and more.

Michael I. Hyman   0-943518-34-2 $23.95
$43.95 w/disk

Hard Disk Management
Updated for the IBM PS/2 and compatibles, this second edition offers a clear and concise explanation of how to use popular software applications packages on a hard disk. Includes detailed techniques for mastering DOS, memory, menus, programs, and files. Includes information on DOS 4.0.

Ralph Blodgett and Emily Rosenthal   0-943518-82-2
$21.95

C Data Base Development
All the tools programmers need for writing C data base programs—with complete, detailed instructions on how to use them. Explains DBMS concepts, C data utilities, the C data compiler, and using C as a data definition language. Includes a billing system program as a sample data base application.

Al Stevens   0-943518-33-4 $23.95
$43.95 w/disk

Turbo C
Everything Turbo C programmers need to get the most out of this fast and powerful programming language. Covers topics and techniques including memory management, ROM BIOS functions, programming screen input/output, and writing memory-resident utility programs in Turbo C.

Al Stevens   0-943518-35-0 $24.95
$44.95 w/disk

*A*vailable where fine books
are sold.